SOLITARY
REFINEMENT

SOLITARY REFINEMENT

THE HIDDEN POWER OF BEING ALONE

ROBB D. THOMPSON

THOMAS NELSON
Since 1798

NASHVILLE DALLAS MEXICO CITY RIO DE JANEIRO BEIJING

Published in Nashville, Tennessee, by Thomas Nelson. Thomas Nelson is a registered0 trademark of Thomas Nelson, Inc.

Thomas Nelson, Inc., titles may be purchased in bulk for educational, business, fund-raising, or sales promotional use. For information, please e-mail SpecialMarkets@ThomasNelson.com.

All anonymous stories in this book are used by permission.

Unless otherwise noted, Scripture quotataions are taken from THE NEW KING JAMES VERSION. © 1982 by Thomas Nelson, Inc. Used by permission. All rights reserved.

Scripture notations marked AMP are from THE AMPLIFIED BIBLE: OLD TESTAMENT. ©1962, 1964 by Zondervan (used by permission); and from THE AMPLIFIED BIBLE: NEW TESTAMENT. © 1958 by the Lockman Foundation (used by permission).

Scripture notations marked MSG are from *The Message* by Eugene H. Peterson. © 1993, 1994, 1995, 1996, 2000. Used by permission of NavPress Publishing Group. All rights reserved.

Scripture notations marked NIV are from the HOLY BIBLE: NEW INTERNATIONAL VERSION®. © 1973, 1978, 1984 by International Bible Society. Used by permission of Zondervan Publishing House. All rights reserved.

Scripture notations marked NLT are from the *Holy Bible*, New Living Translation. © 1996. Used by permission of Tyndale House Publishers, Inc., Wheaton, Illinois 60189. All rights reserved.

Scripture notations marked TLB are from *The Living Bible*. © 1971. Used by permission of Tyndale House Publishers, Inc., Wheaton, Illinois 60189. All rights reserved.

Scripture quotations marked KJV are from the KING JAMES VERSION.

ISBN: 978-1-5995-1029-3

Printed in the United States of America
08 09 10 11 12 13 QW 6 5 4 3 2 1

Solitary Refinement is dedicated to my lovely wife, Linda.
She is not only the love of my life but my greatest source of
strength and reason to pursue heaven's best and place these eternal
truths in print for the transformation of our Christian family.

To Jesus Christ; without His sacrifice, we would all surely perish;

May God touch you eternally as you peruse these pages.

CONTENTS

chapter one

MONUMENTAL MOMENTS

Let me begin with a story that I am sure you can relate with. I'll kill you!" the infuriated woman growled, reddening veins in her neck nearly popping with heated rage.

The Christian mother's heart quickened at the woman's wrath, her next-door neighbor threatening her once again, having used similar savage words countless occasions before. With parents living in another state, her husband swearing that "no woman was going to make him move," the other neighbors refusing to get involved, and her church family perplexed as to a solution, the thirtysomething woman escaped into the lower-level bedroom of her comfortable suburban home, desperate for help. The kids occupied elsewhere, she mused, *I just know He can do it*, acknowledging that only God was capable of rescuing her from the recurrent harassment. But she had to get alone, away from the cable television news, the library novels, the chatter of family, and the voices of her past and present, to sense God's presence. Alone, she knew that change would take place. She was determined to do it; she just had to make the most of these monumental moments alone.

Several decades earlier, not far from that suburban home, a buttery-haired little girl's parents were swept away into their own raucous world of addictions and quarreling. The young child, although physically in the same apartment as her parents, was emotionally detached, miles away from her family of four, numbing feelings and nerve-racking questions plaguing her soul. But strangely, though alone, *she was not!* Someone *was* there. An invisible Someone who was warm, affectionate, inviting, silently guiding, instructing, and mentoring her tender life. But it was only when she slipped past the fray, desperately gliding into those monumental moments alone, that she found more than life itself, literally discovering everything.

In a neighboring state, a young man's smile faded as swiftly as the morning's sunrise: *what would he do now that Mom was gone, his sole emotional support in a family of turmoil?* Alone in his upstairs bedroom, the grieving son had not one tear left to shed. Hearing the traffic drone a few blocks away and the television blast downstairs, with everything stripped away, his anguish lay as raw as a newly opened wound. With nowhere else to turn and no one else upon whom to rely, in sheer desperation, he knelt on the creamy carpet, preparing to receive whatever transformation God could bring, coming face-to-face with his fears, freeing himself to spend life-altering, monumental moments alone.

As contemporary lifestyles embrace endless sporting events, longer work schedules, supplemental schooling, and twenty-four-hour online shopping, it is almost as if being alone has become stigmatized, an oddity reserved solely for hermits and monks. In our culture's flurry of chaotic activity, how can we find time alone and how can we make the most of it after we've succeeded in finding it? And what if it's not as hard as we think?

Regardless of the people who may surround our lives, we are frequently left alone with the feelings, questions, and voices that swirl inside our overloaded minds. Throughout the day and night, we experience these moments alone. Of course, sometimes we pursue time alone by purposely scheduling it at a place and time free of distractions in order to finish a certain project, but what if we could productively utilize these moments when we are alone to truly revolutionize ourselves, our families, neighbors, communities, and eternity as well?

We can do this and more, once we cross the threshold beyond mere solitude into solitary refinement and discover the hidden power of being alone—monumental moments that change everything. Each chapter of this book not only shares notable wisdom on the hidden power of being alone but takes you on a journey through the Bible, highlighting how being alone with God transformed lives of those in the Scriptures. *Enjoy the journey!*

chapter two

VICIOUS VOICES:
ON MY OWN

As infants, most of us enter this life negatively influenced by the vicious voices of sin. Born into a family plagued with failure and hopelessness, my parents were alcoholics and drug abusers long before such addictions had become fashionable. Although Dad was a quiet man, he made it clear that I was unwanted. In fact, the only time he would speak to me was to call me an expletive or say other hurtful words.

As a child, I would lie to my friends about why my father remained home in the middle of the day when everyone else's fathers worked. "Oh, he doesn't go to work this time of the day," I'd fib. Once, I remember telling all the guys that my father was a Major League umpire. When they'd notice my dad was at home, they'd ask, "Why is he home? Isn't this a game day?" Needless to say, it was hard to perpetuate the lie. I was ashamed of my father, and I can honestly say I don't remember him ever telling me he liked me, let alone that he loved me. In recollection, the only time my father ever did anything with my brothers and me was when he and Mom were mulling over the possibility of a divorce. When they separated for a few months, Dad took me to the park. *Once*. It was uneventful, to say the least, but it is a memory I cherished for the entirety of my childhood.

My parents never did divorce, but I could only imagine life improving if they had. On one occasion, I witnessed my father lift up my mother, toss her into the shower, and activate the water. And quite frequently she would pick a fistfight, deliberately seeking anything to satisfy her attention-getting personality.

Overhearing a conversation between my parents one day, my brothers and I nervously exchanged glances. "Look," my father said to my mother, "we've got a little money; what do you think we should do—buy bread, or we should buy beer?"

My mother quickly retorted, "Let's buy beer." And just like that, our family didn't eat.

I learned to hoard cookies in my jacket pockets so I wouldn't go hungry. The school I attended at the time sold peanut butter cookies for two cents each, so every time I had two pennies, I would buy one. Wanting the cookie to last as long as possible, I would munch a little bit at a time, and then return the remnants to my pocket. There were times when I would pull it out and just gaze at it, comforted by the fact that if I could still see it, I still had something to eat. Eventually, I'd finish every last crumb, along with all the cotton pills in the pocket's lining, which I didn't mind because the memory of the cookie was so great.

Due to several factors, my mom was never really a mother to us; she was one of the kids, always trying to be our friend, never assuming the role of parent. Often she would embarrass us, wanting to dance and play with our childhood friends. And when I came home and had to shove garbage out of my way to open the front door, I knew Mother was drunk. Warily opening the door, I would take a peek inside and then hastily close it, walking away in shame.

Since I rarely experienced parental love or care, it's no wonder that at a very young age, I became privy to the evil elements of life. By the time I was six years old, I knew and had even experienced sexual situations that a young child should never encounter. Once, I overheard someone else's parents in bed having sex, which was embarrassing enough, but then I realized one of them (preferring to be with a different partner) was calling their mate by another name. They thought I was asleep, but I was awake, listening to the vicious voices of sin. Sadly, by the age of seven, I was sexually involved with a girl.

One day some of the guys from the neighborhood crowded into the gangway between my house and the neighbor's house and began taunting me: "We know somebody who went to the Audi Home for what you are doing." The Audi Home, by the way, was a juvenile detention center that we all feared. Upon hearing those words, this gut-wrenching feeling of guilt seized me with the force of a heavy club. I hadn't realized that what I was doing was wrong. In that split second, everything that had been innocent about my life became perverted. Those guys intended to scare the hell out of me, but instead, they scared it *into* me. For the first time in my life, I recognized my sinfulness.

That day I realized that I was wrong before God. I felt profoundly ashamed and guilty. When it was time for bed, I walked into my room and got down on my knees. Alone in my room for the next two hours, I asked the Lord to forgive me, pleading, "God, forgive me. I never wanted to do this to You, never! I'm so sorry! Please forgive me."

After those agonizing two hours, it was as though a Voice spoke to me, saying, *Get up, My son. You are forgiven.* When I got up, the guilt was gone and I was able to fall asleep. And after listening to the vicious voices of sin, *alone* and on my own as a seven-year-old boy, I had unexpectedly encountered God for the very first time.

—∞—

In Genesis 28, alone with God one night, Jacob beheld angels trekking back and forth between heaven and earth. And in Exodus 1, alone with God while in a foreign land, Hebrew midwives risked their lives by obeying the Lord's arresting command to save all the male babies, one of whom was Israel's leader and prophet, Moses.

chapter three

ABSOLUTELY ALONE

Like almost everyone who has an encounter with the God of the universe, for the next few months I attempted to live as impeccably as possible. But failing to fully understand what it meant to live for God, I soon retreated into a degraded and perverted lifestyle. I only went to elementary school about three days a week when it was required that I attend five. Eventually my absences resulted in a truant officer visiting our house. When I saw him approach the front door, my brothers and I ran and hid behind the couch so he wouldn't see us in our underwear. I heard Mother open the door and the truant officer ask, "Why aren't your children in school?"

"Because they don't have any clothes to wear," she candidly answered.

The truant officer gave Mother some tickets, and she took us to a big store that looked like a warehouse, filled with shoes, coats, and pants. I'd never seen anything like it in my life. Amazed, I looked around and chose a jacket and a pair of dungarees. I really loved my new clothes. It was the first time I had something new to wear.

I returned to school, proudly sporting my new dungarees. My third-grade teacher, bitter and angry with life, spitefully punished me for my absences by ordering me to drop down upon my hands and knees on the wooden floor behind the piano to sweep away the dirt and trash with a whisk broom.

"Please don't make me go behind the piano," I begged. "It's so dark. Please! These are my new dungarees. Please don't make me go."

Unyielding, she crossly commanded me to get down and clean. After I was finished, she opened the door between the two classrooms and in front of everyone yanked me upright and announced, "You see this boy? He is stupid. He'll never amount to anything. He can't even read." The other children's laughter pierced me like sharp pins as they laughed and laughed and laughed.

In a classroom full of children, I felt utterly and absolutely alone. I was embarrassed, hurt, and angry. I felt it all that day. I had no one at home to discuss it with, no shoulder upon which to cry. There was no one to stand up for me and believe in me, no one to tell me that those demeaning words weren't true. I was absolutely alone with my feelings and tormenting thoughts.

Over time my circumstances changed, but those memories remain. I can honestly say that I do not have any recollection of a positive childhood. Instead, my growing-up years were filled with perversion, hatred, and evil. It was as though a porcupine had shot me full of tiny little holes equal to the number of times people had taken advantage of me. Consequently, I aim to live my life never telling someone anything other than the truth. Never will I hurt anyone with words like those that hurt me. I have learned that words are very powerful—more deadly than weapons that strike only once, because words can be replayed in our minds over and over again. I have been wounded a thousand times over by vicious, hurting words.

By age thirteen I was an alcoholic, and by sixteen I regularly used drugs. A nobody going nowhere fast, while a senior in high school, I met the girl who would become my wife, Linda. She attended an all-girls' Catholic school and happened to be the happiest person I'd ever met. And since I was miserable, she was exactly what I was looking for.

Although I didn't have much going for me, Linda's parents tolerated me because I was always respectful. There would even be times when I'd stand in front of them stoned out of my brain, but I always remained respectful. They knew I loved their daughter and that she loved me. I never involved them in my problems, thinking, *Why make them pay for what somebody else did to me?*

One day Linda and I began to argue when she said something that changed my life forever: "You say you don't want to be like your parents, but you're exactly like them."

I called her a derogatory name and bristled. "I can kick your rear end, so let's not even go there."

But she repeated, "You're just like them."

Defensive, I asked, "How do you figure?"

"Your parents do it with booze; you do it with drugs. It's the same thing."

"That's easy for you to say," I protested, but I knew she was right. I didn't believe there was anything I could do to avert my eventual downfall, so I attempted to free myself by marrying her. I erroneously thought that if I married someone who was happy, then I would be happy too. I didn't yet understand that people can't make you happy, but people can definitely make you miserable.

Linda and I were married by the age of twenty-one. I remember that day well, but not for the typical reasons people usually remember their wedding day. In reality, it was a very unhappy day for all of us. As Linda's father escorted her down the wedding aisle, she saw me standing in the front of the church, prepared to marry her. Shocked that I actually showed up, she exclaimed, "Dad, he came!" Horrified, her father tried to keep his composure in front of everyone. And today, if you were to look through the wedding photos, you would think my closest friend just died.

After the wedding, things got worse instead of better. Since I didn't have to spend any more energy lying to gain Linda's love, I was suddenly free to do whatever I wanted to do, whenever I wanted to do it. I thought my life would improve when I got married, but instead, it began to seriously deteriorate.

At the outset of our marriage, my uncle, who had purchased an investment home, approached me with an offer, saying, "If you and Linda would like to, you can move into this house. Whatever amount of money you put into it, I'll give it back to you when you move. Or you can just take it over and buy it; it doesn't matter to me."

I jumped at the chance, responding, "Sure, that'd be great!" I really liked this particular uncle, who was my mother's brother. So Linda and I finished the entire house for him. We painted and installed carpet, appliances, and furniture. Nevertheless, I needed a job to support us and eventually found one as a property manager. Since I was required to live on the property, I explained to my uncle that I needed to move out of the house because I had to make some money. Handing him all the receipts from the home improvements Linda and I had made, I explained that we now needed the money to help us move.

"I'm not giving you anything," he snarled.

"But you told me you would!" I protested.

"Yeah, but now I'm just not going to."

Since my uncle owned the house, I had no leverage to acquire the funds he had promised. I was young, had very little money, and worst of all, my favorite uncle had betrayed me. So I took the property management position where I was in charge of about eleven hundred units, but only ended up working there for a few short months. (During that time, however, I discovered that the owners were using me as a pawn to break their union.)

"Go in and talk to the sales department. You need to motivate these salespeople," came their brusque orders. After I did as they said, they demanded, "Go talk to the maintenance department." So I reprimanded the maintenance workers: "Look, we need you to get your work done. You're not doing it as fast as you should."

When the maintenance manager heard my sharp reprimand, he lifted his hammer, pounded it on the table, and asserted, "Listen, you punk, what do you think you're going to tell *me*? I've been here twelve years. The owners have made me pull old refrigerators out of apartments and used appliances off the walls to install in other apartments, just because they didn't want to buy anything. So don't talk to me about what we need to do. My guys are working as hard as they can."

That's when it dawned on me what the owners were doing. Feeling used, I decided to quit. Unfortunately, at that point in time, an ex-con lived across the hall from Linda and me. I really liked this guy because he was a race car driver. We'd often go out and take drives together. As we were walking to the store one day, he casually remarked, "We're going to rob this store."

"*Rob this store?*" I was shocked.

"Yeah, every Saturday at two o'clock, Brinks comes by and picks up anywhere from a hundred to two hundred thousand dollars cash. I've already planned it out."

"I don't want to," I said.

"All you've got to do is drive," my neighbor replied, explaining how I could drive the getaway car, which happened to be the fairly expensive one that I owned.

The week ticked by, and though I had agreed to the plan, I really began sweating it. Sunday, Monday, Tuesday . . . I'd catch myself thinking, *you know you can't do it; this is really stupid.*

Saturday finally came, and we were about ready to go when I finally told him, "Look, I just can't do this."

He said, "All right. No big deal."

"No big deal?" I asked in disbelief. After tormenting myself all week long! But that's the way people make you feel sometimes—you're going through hell inside your head wondering if you hurt the person by something you did or said, only to discover later on that he or she didn't care one bit about it anyway. Afterward you're left thinking, *you mean, I was so much deeper into the care of this thing than you were?*

A short while later, my ex-con friend and I were hanging out when he suddenly said, "You know something? You could make a lot of money."

"I could?"

"Yeah, and I'll tell you how to do it." This guy had spent a long time in San Quentin, you see, so he knew all the ropes. He advised,

"Work for an import company, and you'll have a lot of inventory in your office. Then here's what you do: tell the police the equipment in your office was stolen, and it belonged to you."

And that's how my ex-con neighbor ensnared me, not with a store robbery, but on a counterfeit claim. Once I heard his idea, I made the poor and regretful decision to act upon his words, words that had the power to kill more than the cruelest weapons known to man.

From ruthless childhood humiliation, to the betrayal of my favorite uncle, to being used by the superiors of my property management position, to listening to a wily neighbor and ex-con, in all these situations I found myself absolutely alone, desperately searching for someone, anyone, to guide and point me in the right direction toward the proper path.

—⁂—

In Leviticus 9, alone with God at the altar, Aaron killed a calf and instituted the priesthood. And in Numbers 1, alone with God in the tabernacle, Moses received the assignment to take a census of Israel; while in Deuteronomy 5, separated from the rest of the world and alone before God, Israel was reminded of the Ten Commandments.

chapter four

SOLD INTO SLAVERY

At Chicago's annual Consumer Electronics Show, I was inter-viewed for a position at an import company. Even though I didn't have any experience in that field, they hired me. Married only eighteen months, I found myself working in downtown Chicago, importing audio equipment from Japan. But when I landed the job, I also landed smack-dab in the worst perversion I could ever imagine. During office hours, any employee could do whatever, to whomever, whenever he or she desired. I worked only three hours a day, high on drugs, making a lot of money, with a secretary who constantly flirted with me. True to my ex-con neighbor's prediction, I saw the opportunity to steal and I took it . . . and to my amazement, I never got caught.

I thought I was in control of my life, but I didn't realize that through living such an unbridled lifestyle, I had been sold into slavery to depraved habits and relationships, living with mounting guilt and shame. I despised the man I was becoming. Here I was, scamming the company while trying to convince myself that I wasn't wrong or corrupt for doing so. Deep down, I knew that life wasn't supposed to be about using people.

During this time in my life, seething hatred for my uncle simmered deep in my mind. What he did to me replayed bitterly inside my soul, and my hatred toward him began to flare, like a raging fire. It was so bad that I began to be angry at life itself. I truly didn't want others to suffer as a result of my problem, so I tried to suppress my anger, but suppressing my anger eventually drove me out of my mind.

Driving home from work one day, all my subconscious fears converged in my consciousness. Normally I was able to get through difficult days with a miniscule amount of destruction, but on this particular day, all the worries about my relationships, work, people's perceptions of me, and questions about my future jointly sprang into my mind. I felt defenseless because for the first time I just couldn't keep the panic away. Fears, worry, and depressing thoughts continued to bombard me. At that moment, I realized that I was going crazy!

Voices raged like furious waves inside my mind as I had no fewer than five conversations going on in my head simultaneously. One voice was stating, *you're a failure; that's all you'll ever be*. Another voice was telling me, *maybe you should take a walk across the street*, to which a third voice replied, *no, no, don't do that*. The second voice protested, *I said he should go across the street. Why are you telling him not to go across the street?* The voices replayed inside my head. At one point, I blurted out, "Would the real Robb Thompson please stand up?" But nobody did.

Somehow I made it safely home. When I arrived, I announced to Linda, "Honey, I love you, but I'm leaving. I don't know if I'll ever come back, so I just want to say good-bye."

Linda broke down and cried, although she wasn't completely surprised. You see, she had married me thinking our relationship would only last a year, and we'd already made it six months longer than she had predicted. Now she realized there was nothing she could do to stop me. I didn't pack before I left, because I didn't care about any of my belongings. I didn't care about anything. Linda didn't know where I was going or if she'd ever see me again.

Tired of bearing the anger toward my uncle, I asked myself, *do I really want to travel down Hatred Boulevard for the rest of my life?* I decided it was better for me to openly confront my uncle (even though one of us would lose) than to continue to seethe against him in anger. After I left Linda, I drove to my uncle's house to kill him.

I found him in his basement. It was my desperate desire to intimidate him and cause him pain, just like he had done to me. So the two of us started talking, but we didn't get very far. Out of nowhere, something happened. Suddenly I was aware of God's overwhelming love for me. It was as though God had revealed my ungodly motive and His love for me at the same time. Just like that, I couldn't go through with killing my uncle. I knew hurting him would be horribly wrong. Sometime later, after repenting and entering into relationship with God, I read an explanation of what happened to me that night: "Test my motives and my heart. For I am always aware of your unfailing love" (Ps. 26:2–3 NLT).

Instead of killing my uncle, I simply drove away. Having no control of what was happening inside of me, I put one hundred and eighty miles on my jeep that night. *Alone*, with nowhere else to go, I drove back home. But those haunting voices continued for three months—a span of time in which I rarely ate or slept. Every night I would pace the floor and then drag myself to work the next morning in utter exhaustion. Looking for any means of relief, I decided to stop taking drugs and began to heavily consume alcohol, hoping the voices would stop. Tormented, I yearned for even thirty minutes of peace of mind.

As I was driving one day, a voice said, *you want all of this to be over?*

"Yes!" I agreed.

Another voice said, *all you need to do is pull the wheel to the left really hard, and this will all be over.* Although my left hand fought my right hand, my right hand would not allow my left hand to kill myself. Linda knew about my struggle with suicidal thoughts, but she didn't understand it. When I would confide in friends that something was wrong with me, they would say, "What are you talking about? There's nothing wrong with you. You've got a pretty wife. You've got as much money as you want. You've got a pretty secretary. Man, you've got the greatest stuff going on in the world. You've got it made."

My reply was, "If you think I've got it all, you have little more than nothing, because I'm an empty man."

As the voices in my mind grew louder and louder, Linda and I decided to throw a party. We thought that a room filled with other people's voices would drown out the ones in my head. But regardless of how many people I surrounded myself with, I couldn't escape the crazy thoughts plaguing my mind. Once again I was *alone*, even in the midst of a throng of people. Observing our guests—fifteen or twenty of them were smoking pot, drinking, sliding down the walls and lying all over the place—I soon realized I was the only person there who wasn't incapacitated. Alone in the hub of the party, I suddenly shouted, "The voices are still here. Go away!" But to no avail; they wouldn't leave. The voices continued day after day, and night after grueling night. I was hopeless and on the verge of committing suicide. There was simply no other viable option.

It even got to the point where I would actually feel the voices that were talking to and influencing other people. The person didn't think the voices were there, but somehow I would recognize each person who followed these voices' commands. I was scared and had no way of stopping what I was experiencing. Continually I blamed myself, thinking, *well, it's got to be me. I'm the one that's got the problem.*

When I couldn't bear the torment any longer, I quit my job. My boss essentially chased me down Michigan Avenue, yelling, "Where are you goin'? Come back! I need you!"

Looking over my shoulder, I shouted, "I'm going crazy, and I'm going without you."

This time I knew I was in some major trouble; I had hit my wit's end. My office downtown was near Holy Name Cathedral, one of the most prominent Catholic churches in Chicago. Entering the building, I beheld five-foot statues lining the walls. Strolling up to the second pew, I saw a gigantic crucifix on the front wall before me. I dropped to my knees and cried out to God, "Help me! I don't know what to do. Please help me."

Nothing happened. The voices remained.

After I closed the gigantic eighteen to twenty-foot brass doors behind me, the Voice spoke, the same Voice I'd heard as a little child. Now it calmly soothed, *hold on. Everything's going to be all right.* Suddenly my worry seemed to vanish. Dread disappeared into thin air. Although the voices remained, the worry was gone. I still heard the other voices in my head, but I no longer was controlled by fear.

The moment I admitted my need for help, while spending time

alone with God, He hastily responded. Our churches today are filled with Christians who live in complete denial. Many mistakenly deny that they have a problem. But there I was, recognizing that I had been sold into slavery and running to God, screaming, "I'm broken; I'm broken; I'm broken! Please fix me!"

One of the greatest things anyone will ever accomplish in life is to stop the voices that plague him. Granted, this is not always done alone, but it is at the place of *being alone* that one must refuse to buckle under pressure and reach toward God.

—⁂—

In Joshua 1, alone with God following Moses' death, Joshua was authorized to seize the Promised Land for the Hebrew nation. And in Judges 6, alone with God in the threshing floor, the Angel of the LORD spoke to Gideon; while in Ruth 1, alone in the world save for God and her mother-in-law Naomi, Ruth humbled herself, thereby creating a hopeful future.

chapter five

OCTOBER OUTCRY

With the intensity of a wildfire that could not be extinguished, throughout the summer and into the fall of that year, the battle in my mind continued to rage. By October, I finally had to admit I was in desperate need of help. On October 4, I went to a psychiatrist who diagnosed me with ambiguous anxiety, which simply meant I was demon possessed and extremely worried about it. By 11:15 a.m., I was a patient in the mental ward of a local hospital. As the door locked ominously behind me, for one brief minute I felt safe, protected from the outside world where I couldn't hurt myself or anyone else.

While in the hospital, I began socializing with some of the other mental ward patients. The paranoid-schizophrenics in the ward accused me of spying on them, Jesus lived down the hall, and the lady in the room next door talked to the Virgin Mary. Needless to say, there were some pretty interesting people there!

Before long I was elected president of the loony bin. As president, I called weekly meetings to discuss the circumstances of various patients. I'd hear typical complaints such as, "I don't like this," "I don't like that," and "I don't like the food," to which I'd promise, "We're going to take care of this," "I'll take care of that," and "Give her two Jell-Os tonight instead of one."

In the particular facility where I found myself, patients were only permitted five-day stays. Although slated for eventual state lockup, for some reason I became their longest-standing patient, remaining at the facility for a whopping forty-one days. During my visit, I kept noticing a certain orderly, wondering what was so different about this fellow. Back then the only way I could laugh was to ridicule other people, so I sauntered around making fun of just about everyone. What a rotten life! But when I ridiculed this one particular orderly, he would just smile.

Halfway into my extended stay, the orderly asked me, "Where would you go if you died today?"

"I'd go to heaven," I replied in heady confidence.

"Really," he said, clearly not believing me. "Why?"

"Beause I'm a good person. I don't want to hurt anybody, including myself. That's one of the reasons I'm here."

The orderly continued, "Why would Jesus have to die for the sins of the world if people could get to heaven by being good?"

I was stumped. "That's a good question," I admitted. "I've never heard that before."

The orderly then shared the gospel with me. I listened to these words intently, captivated by what he was relaying. He even gave me a Bible to read.

Finally alone, on the night of October 28, 1975, I stayed up as long as I could in order to read the Bible. I didn't want to put it down. I knelt and repented, the words becoming an outcry of my heart, "Jesus, I want to be born again. I've sinned against heaven, and I've sinned against You. I am guilty, and I need Your grace. I don't want to do anything bad again. I'm finished, Jesus. You're Lord; I'm not. You're God; I'm not. You're King; I'm not. I've blown my life. I've blown everything around me. I'm about to wreck everybody I've ever known. Jesus, I make You the Lord of my life. Be my King. I repent, and I take myself off the throne and I put You on it." That night I went to bed at eleven thirty, desperately clutching that Bible.

The interesting thing about this was that staying up late was totally unheard of since there were very strict rules in the mental ward. Patients who didn't go to bed by eleven o'clock were forcibly strapped to a table, given a shot, and put into a straightjacket. Miraculously, that night no one said a thing. Waking up the next morning, I was a brand-new person. That day the haircut lady pushed her cart down the hallway and stopped by to visit me. I instructed her, "I want you to cut my beard short enough so I can shave it. And then I want you to cut my hair."

She warned, "Your wife might not like that."

"What I'm going to tell Linda, she's going to like much less than that." So she cut my hair, and we shaved off my beard.

Observing me for a couple of weeks after my conversion, the doctor changed my diagnosis from ambiguous anxiety to a deep character disorder. Later that week he released me from the hospital with this warning, "All I can do is help you get over the hump. Nine out of ten people like you return every year. So I'll see you next year."

With great assurance I responded, "No, sir. You won't see me in here again. God has delivered me!"

I slowly realized that when I had spent that night alone, desperately seeking God and finding Him, I had encountered the power necessary to alter my life. But it all began while I was alone, starting with this October outcry from my soul.

—⁂—

In I Samuel 1, alone with God in the temple, Hannah prayed for a son and was soon with child; while in 2 Samuel 12, alone with God following the consequences of his sin, David worshiped the Lord. In 1 Kings 3, alone with God at Gibeon, the Lord asked Solomon about his greatest desire; in 2 Kings 20, alone with God in desperate prayer, King Hezekiah was granted fifteen additional years of life.

chapter six

INTENSIFIED INTENTS
OF THE HEART

W hen the hospital attendants finally opened the door to release me, I didn't realize they had just opened the door not only to my physical freedom but to my emotional freedom as well.

After I was released from the hospital, Linda and I lived with her parents. We didn't have very much at the time, and they were kind enough to allow us to spend a few months with them. And so we stayed with them as I was putting my life in order. I didn't care what I had to sacrifice as long as I could live right before God. It was irrelevant what it cost me; I only cared about God and what *He* thought about me. Every waking moment I thought solely about Him. I desired nothing more than to intensify my relationship with Him and read His Word.

Every night I would leave the house and walk about a half mile to a church building that had an illuminated, forty-foot-high cross. I would kneel before that cross and meditate on the goodness and greatness of God. It was the cross that had made me new; the cross that had provided a brand-new life. I had been separated from death, and although the cross represented death for Jesus, it represented life for me.

After I'd been a Christian for only forty-five days, Linda and I were invited to her boss's Christmas party. Linda was a schoolteacher, and I wanted to attend the gathering to thank the principal for his kindness to us while I was in the hospital. On the day of the party, Linda's boss stood at the door greeting everyone as they entered. I shook his hand and said, "I just want to thank you for everything you did for my wife and me. Without you, I would never have made it. I'm so grateful."

"Aw, it's no big deal," he cheerfully voiced. "Come on in, just enjoy yourself."

Stepping in to enjoy the party, I somehow couldn't have any fun. Inside that room, I fell into the greatest slump I'd been in since the day I checked into the mental ward. Every negative thought from which Jesus had released me reintroduced itself to me at that party. My mind was being ambushed, and my only recourse was to read the Word of God. Though I was surrounded by people, I felt completely alone—just as I had when my father called me those derogatory names, when the neighborhood boys confronted me, and when my teacher said I'd never amount to anything. And once again, no one on earth could help me when I faced one of the most difficult moments of my life. The problem, you see, was not external; it was internal. And I had to fight this on my own using the weapon of God's Word.

How will I make it through the night? I worried. I knew of only one thing that could help me. Finding the table farthest away from the crowd, I sat down and began reading my Bible, which I took with me everywhere in those days. Linda spotted me and began to complain, "Come on, will you please stop it? You can't do this. These people are watching you."

"If you think I'm acting badly now," I warned, "just wait and see how I'll act if you pull me away from my Bible. I don't know what else to do here."

So there I sat, my eyes glued to the pages of the Bible. It seemed as though every time I glanced up from the Scriptures, the voices would return; insanity was glaring directly in my face. But every time I peered back into the Word of God, the voices ceased; freedom extended its gracious hand. Meditating on what God said was the only way I made it through that night, as well as the many difficult nights that followed.

In the days ahead, I continued to read my Bible every moment I could. When I'd been a Christian three months, I read Ephesians 4:28: "Let him who stole steal no longer, but rather let him labor, working with his hands what is good, that he may have something to give him who has need." I contemplated this truth, thinking, *I need to work with my hands*. So that's when I got a job driving a school bus.

Accustomed to making a lot of money working downtown, I had to adjust to making a little money driving a school bus. Four hours a day, from 5:30 a.m. to 7:30 a.m., then again from 2:30 p.m. to 4:30 p.m., I would drive the bus. In the hours between, I would read the Bible. The Holy Spirit was speaking to me so much that I actually underlined almost every verse in the Bible.

At this point, Jesus was very real to me. He would seemingly enter my room in the morning, greeting me with, *I've been waiting for you to get up*.

I'd answer, "Oh, Jesus, it's nice to see You."

Then He would say, *I have something I want you to do for Me today.*

"Really?" I'd ask.

Yes, I have a person I want you to talk to.

I'd reply, "Yes, I'd be happy to. It would be my pleasure."

Even though Jesus wasn't physically present in my room, I knew exactly where and how He was standing. I could talk to Him as though I was talking to a visible person. Then, every workday morning, Jesus would accompany me to the bus. He would board the bus and stand in the wheel well where the children would ascend the stairs. But one day Jesus didn't seem to stand in the wheel well anymore. He walked all the way up the steps and sat down in the row right behind me. Since He'd never done that before, I grew extremely nervous. Silent for twenty minutes, I experienced more fear when God wasn't talking to me than when five conversations were going on in my head all at once.

Finally, He said, *I want you to do something for Me.*

Relieved, I replied, "Yes, sir."

I want you to return to the insurance company you embezzled money from and tell them what you did.

Frightened, I pleaded, "Jesus, I love You, but I don't want to go to jail! I love You. You forgave me of my sins. In 2 Corinthians 5:17, You said that if any man be in Christ, he's a new creature; old things are passed away."

Jesus didn't respond. For the first time since I'd been saved, the presence of God was not there. In its place, all of the fear I had once known dolefully returned.

For weeks I wrestled within. *How could I face the insurance company executives? But how could I not do as Jesus asked, since I had already made up my mind to follow Him?*

Alone with my thoughts, I plummeted emotionally. But it is in times like these that character is formed, that who you are is tested and defined. Looking for help, I decided to approach an ex-con at the church I attended, saying, "I know you were an armed robber. Tell me, what do you do when you want to pay people back for what you did?"

He replied, "That's easy. I get the money, put it in an envelope, and I write a note saying, 'Hi. I robbed you at gunpoint. I'm sorry. I'm a Christian now. I hope I didn't scare you too much. Here's your money back. I've repented.'"

Delighted, I exclaimed, "Eureka! That's everything I needed to know!"

But then a Voice I had not heard for weeks said to me, *That's not what I asked you to do.*

Miserable, I called an attorney who had once helped me dodge a DUI. Apprehensively I inquired, "Can you help me out? I know you're not going to understand this, but I want to go back to an insurance company to tell them I embezzled money."

Astonished, he asked, "Why would you do that?"

I continued, "Look, I just need to do it, okay? Can you help me out?"

"Well," he responded curiously, "tell me the story."

So I told him a little bit about what happened. He replied, "I think we can do this. We're probably going to have to bribe somebody, but we can get this done. Don't worry about it."

"Wait a minute," I said. "Let me tell *you* something. No more bribes, no more lies, no more cheating, no more stealing."

Skeptically he stated, "Well then, I don't know what's going to happen. You know, you could go to jail."

"I know," I admitted, pausing a moment to explain. "It is crazy to talk to you about this. Forget it."

By this time, Linda and I had moved from her parents' home into an apartment, and we were hosting a Bible study in our home. Our pastor's son attended, and one day I dared to confide my predicament to him. He listened and then said, "I know somebody who went to jail for that."

Overhearing us, my wife added, "I'll wait for you. Maybe the Lord wants you to have a jail ministry."

Incredulous, I exclaimed, "I don't want a jail ministry! I don't want to go to jail!"

So I decided to see my pastor. After listening to my story, he said, "Here is the name of an attorney who might be able to help you. He owns a big firm in downtown Chicago."

I thanked him and left to call the attorney. I explained my situation and then asked, "Can you help me? I'm in trouble."

He responded, "I'd like to help you, but unfortunately I'm very busy right now. A lot of people are in trouble."

"Yes, but you have to help me."

"I'm sorry, but I'm completely booked right now," the lawyer insisted.

"Please, please! What am I going to do? You're not working for me; you're working for Jesus!"

I apparently captured his attention, because he answered, "For that reason, I'll consider your case."

Relieved, I said, "Listen to me. I would rather be a free man behind bars than be a prisoner walking the streets."

The lawyer then explained, "I'll take your case if you tell me it's all right if the insurance company wants to put you in jail."

I said, "It's okay. I don't care. No matter what, I'm not living without God."

He asked, "What's the name of the insurance company?"

After I told him, he said, "Do you understand that's an English-owned company?"

I said, "Yes, sir."

He continued, "I have a friend who works for that company. He has an office right inside this building."

Excitedly I questioned, "He *does?*"

"Yes, he has a Bible study that I go to."

"He *does?*"

"Yes. Give me a little time to talk to him."

I didn't hear from the lawyer for several agonizing days. Certain the FBI was coming to seize me, periodically I would step outside of my apartment and scan the area, certain they were surrounding my building. Then I began thinking, *what am I going to do? That attorney isn't going to call me back. Now I'm on my own.* I could picture my jail ministry on its way.

Finally, the attorney called me. He said, "The insurance company wants to talk to you."

I agreed, reminding my lawyer that I honestly didn't care what happened, as long as I obeyed what Jesus wanted me to do.

On the prearranged day, I drove to the insurance company. When I arrived, the secretary escorted me to a glass-walled room overlooking downtown Chicago. All alone, I scanned the room and noticed a huge desk with a Bible lying on top. Walking over to the desk, I patted the Bible and said, "I'm glad you're here."

At that moment, the door opened. An insurance company executive and my attorney strode inside. Extending his hand, the executive introduced himself and said, "I am the head claims adjuster for this entire company. In the hundred-year history of our company, no one has ever attempted to make restitution."

I responded, "Please, don't celebrate me. I'm not here because you caught me. I'm not here because I'm guilty. I'm not here for any reason except that Jesus Christ told me to come and tell you what I did."

For an hour I talked, and for an hour he took notes on everything I said about the embezzlement and my radical transformation. A cigarette dangled precariously from his lower lip when he finally opened his mouth to say, "Wow! That is some story."

I agreed, "Yes, that's some story all right."

Abruptly he asked, "Okay, where's the money?"

"I don't have it," I once again truthfully replied. "God never told me that part."

"You want to make restitution and you have no money?"

"I brought a little bit. Here's the money I do have."

He looked at my little pile of money and then said, "It's okay, I already wrote it off anyway. No big deal."

"No, please! I don't want you to forgive me of this debt. I want to repay every penny I stole. Right now I'm only driving a school bus, and it's hard for us to pay our bills. May I pay you back every month?"

He agreed to monthly payments, stating, "Pay me every month. I'm not going to charge you any interest, but be sure to pay me back as soon as you're able."

Aware of my attorney seated behind me, I started wondering, *how much do I owe him for all the hours he invested on my behalf?* Knowing I owed him a lot, I asked him the amount. To my surprise, tears were streaming down his face.

I repeated the question, "How much money do I owe you?"

He said, "You don't owe me a thing. I've been a Christian all my life, and you've been a Christian for only three months. I've slipped away from God and am so ashamed of myself."

Before my very eyes, my attorney was reconciling with God. He began to pour out his heart about his family and what happened on his father's deathbed. He asked, "Will you pray with me?" We prayed, and then he said, "Because of what you've done, I'm appointing Jesus as Senior Partner of my law firm. I will not do anything without Jesus' approval."

I didn't understand his attorney jargon, but I did understand that during the hour when I was talking to the adjuster, God was talking to my attorney.

When our meeting was over, I didn't leave the building alone. Instead, my attorney honored me by escorting me out of the high-rise onto the busy Chicago street. I didn't deserve it; I was just a twenty-two-year-old kid who didn't know a thing.

I asked the Lord, "Why did You want me to do that? You had already forgiven me for embezzling."

Because no one but you could bring My son [the attorney] back to Me, He answered. *It took you to get him back.*

It took several years, but I eventually paid back everything I owed the insurance company. I guarantee, if I had held on to the idea that I didn't have to obey God because He had already forgiven me, not only would my attorney have been in trouble, but I wouldn't be where I am in life today, training and mentoring individuals and governmental leaders around the globe to pursue personal excellence and maximize their God-given potential.

But my willingness to obey God was forged in the moments when

Jesus tutored me privately—altering, reconstructing, and refining the intensified intents of my heart.

—∞—

In 1 Chronicles 17, alone with God, it was revealed to the prophet Nathan that David's throne would be established forever; in 2 Chronicles 15, alone with God, the prophet Azariah revealed such encouraging words from the Lord that King Asa removed idols from all the land. And in Ezra 10, while alone with God in His temple, a large assembly joined Ezra in repenting before the Lord.

chapter seven

TRANSFORMING THOUGHTS

Over the years I have come to understand that what is seen isn't necessarily true; it's as misleading as a desert mirage. Countless men and women say they love God and live a life of victory in front of others while they privately exist in mental, physical, and spiritual torment. For the first five years after I was saved, I tried to become a nice guy, attempting to be a person who walks freely, living a simple yet isolated life.

Many people would have wholeheartedly agreed that I was the nicest Christian they knew. Linda and I attended church every time the doors were open; we tithed and did all of the things people do when they're believers. But I was frequently depressed by the negative thoughts I still battled. My life was failing, and I didn't know what to do—that is, until the day I discovered the answer that took me by surprise. That was the day I met a man who introduced me to true Christianity. While Linda was at a women's retreat, I decided to attend a church picnic, and that's where everything exploded. I met a man who dismantled my entire theology and all I claimed to believe. This man humbled me, but in the process of challenging my beliefs, he greatly altered much of which I had previously learned.

I knew my Bible and could quote hundreds of passages, but this guy really *knew* the Scriptures. I knew Bible stories, but he knew the Word of God. In my immaturity as a believer, I had constructed a set of standards that supported my position of unbelief. Yet this man, skillfully wielding the Scriptures, demonstrated how foolish much of my belief system had been. This fellow used Scripture to explain that I had to decide to let God's Word transform me. He helped me understand that if I was going to be transformed, it was only the Scriptures that could change me—mentally, emotionally, and spiritually.

CHANGE OCCURS WHEN YOU EMBRACE THE WORDS YOU NEVER WANTED TO HEAR

We have all witnessed people skirting the issues, haven't we? Whether it's a question-dodging television interview with a politician or parents asking their children, "Now which one of you did it?", most people dodge the issues, comfortably settling into the gray smog of a compromising lifestyle instead of choosing to live in the untainted world of the pure in heart. Mistakenly thinking it's acceptable to exist in the gray, they wait for God's mercy to pick up the pieces of their bad decisions.

During our conversation, this man wholeheartedly exposed my false beliefs, showing me how to stop living in the bondage of a self-indulgent lifestyle. I returned home and crashed on an oversized, brown-checkered pillow. Still lying there when Linda returned home, she said, "You look horrible. What happened?"

"I've been to war," I confessed. "And I lost."

Sharing with Linda how the man had blown away everything I had believed, I admitted, "I don't like him, but he was right."

He had labored with me in love, not allowing me to skirt the issues, but teaching me from the Word of God. This man taught me that what Christ did for me went beyond salvation to a new identity. Second Corinthians 5:17 became even more real to me: "Therefore, if anyone is in Christ, he is a new creation; old things have passed away; behold, all things have become new."

The man had explained that God's Word contained everything I needed for healing, prosperity, peace, and more. After our conversation, God's Word came alive to me all over again. I saw promises that God wanted to keep in my life, and I recognized that I would receive what He promised if I learned how to walk by faith and trust Him at His Word. Finally, I admitted, "You know what, honey? I can't help but think he was right."

At that moment, my life was completely transformed. I admitted that I had been looking for the absence of depression instead of looking for God's power presented in His written Word. It was then that I stopped reading the Bible just to demonstrate that I knew the stories about Zacchaeus, blind Bartimaeus, the Syrophoenician woman, and the woman at the well. Since the Bible was written for me to follow, I started reading it to change me.

Change Occurs When You Let God's Word Transform You

Romans 12:2 says, "Don't copy the behavior and customs of this world, but *let God transform you into a new person by changing the way you think*" (NLT; emphasis added).

I desperately desired to overcome my bad habits and the voices that still tried to overtake me. I wanted to think the way God thinks. Isaiah gave us the greatest challenge of all when he spoke God's words: "As the heavens are higher than the earth, so are My ways higher than your ways, and My thoughts than your thoughts" (Isa. 55:9).

In the meantime, I began going to the church the man attended and joined his house group, where he taught me how to believe and stand upon the Scriptures. He taught me how to create confessions (faith declarations) formulated directly from the Word of God. For example, when I felt emotionally weak, I would read, "'My grace is sufficient for you, for my power is made perfect in weakness.' Therefore I will boast all the more gladly about my weaknesses, so that Christ's power may rest on me" (2 Cor. 12:9–10 NIV). Then I would say, "When I am weak, God's power rests on me."

Through a series of events, I took a job with a package-delivery service where I worked harder and faster than the other employees, delivering more packages in less time than any of them. While driving to the delivery destinations on my route, I was able to listen to the Word of God approximately ten hours a day. The Scriptures began to transform my life because I was purposely listening to change the way I thought. I had to completely reprogram my mind, erasing the hard drive and rebuilding a new one from the bottom up so that all of my ways of deducing truth and assimilating situations changed.

When arriving at a church that was on my route each day, I would pull over and descend the steps into the church basement. Right there, I would literally pace the floors alone with God, praying and confessing specific scriptures to transform specific trouble spots in my life. I clearly remember one particular day when I experienced a moment that redefined my life. For several days I had trouble trusting God, so I confessed 2 Corinthians 5:7: "For we walk by faith, not by sight" when it finally gave up its nectar to me. On this day, 2 Corinthians 5:7 became who I was. While I was walking, I repeated over and over: "I walk by faith and not by sight. I walk by faith and not by sight. I walk by faith and not by sight."

All of a sudden, I was no longer trying to force something to happen. Inside of me, it happened—I *knew* I was walking by faith. No longer was I merely *saying* I walk by faith in an effort to try to walk by faith; now I was saying I walk by faith because I actually was! Jesus explained this kind of transformation: "For out of the abundance of the heart his mouth speaks" (Luke 6:45).

Most people don't stay with a verse long enough for it to change them. God's Word will not do you any good until it completely permeates your core. For this to happen, you must repeat the verse until it fully dominates your thoughts. When you begin to confess a verse, you won't see immediate change in your thoughts and behavior because initially the verse works invisibly on the inside of you. It is no different than a seed. A seed is planted within where you can't observe its growth. But the moment finally arrives when God's seed begins to sprout and supernaturally changes a person from the inside out.

Most people don't understand the power that is infused into them the moment they intentionally choose to be alone with God, allowing His Word, His power, and His presence to penetrate their hearts.

The wise choice of getting alone with God and His Word is the key to personal transformation.

Before my conversation with the man at the church picnic, I knew that I truly loved God. But loving Him didn't change me. Loving God does not transform a person's life; a person is only transformed by renewing his or her mind to the Word of God. Loving God is important and necessary, but an experiential love for God apart from His Word will not change you. It is the consistent meditation on His words that transforms the way you think, feel, and act.

But few of us truly realize that transforming thoughts are primarily begun while getting alone primarily with God.

—⁓—

In Nehemiah 1, alone with the God of heaven, Nehemiah was burdened to rebuild the broken wall surrounding Jerusalem. In Esther 4, alone with God, Queen Esther fasted and prayed, trusting Him for a favorable outcome in regard to the future of the Jews. In Job 42, alone with God, Job realized that God could do everything, and in Psalms, after being alone with God, one hundred and fifty beautiful songs and praises were created to uplift believers around the world throughout history.

chapter eight

MENTORING MY MIND

Scotsman Eric H. Liddell was an athlete whose exclusive aim was to please God. In the movie *Chariots of Fire*, he explains to his sister, Jenny, why he feels compelled to run in the Olympics: "I believe God made me for a purpose, but He also made me fast. And when I run I feel His pleasure." After winning the men's 400-meter race at the 1924 Olympic Games held in Paris, he surrendered fame and fortune to serve God by becoming a missionary to China.

Eric Liddell knew what would please God, and the more time I study the Scriptures, the more I, too, discover exactly what pleases and satisfies God. If God liked carrot juice and you served Him orange juice, why would you expect Him to be pleased? If God wanted you to exchange your thoughts for His thoughts and you accepted every random thought that trudged through your mind, would you expect God to be content?

We Cannot Earn God's Love, but We Must Earn God's Pleasure

Would you like to know why many believers routinely need to hear that God loves them? It's because "those who are living the life of the flesh [catering to the appetites and impulses of their carnal nature] cannot please or satisfy God, or be acceptable to Him" (Rom. 8:8 AMP). I cannot please God as long as I am compromising, can I? So it is important not to merely assume what pleases God but to know for certain, and you can discover that in His Word.

Often people believe they can get everything they want without giving God what *He* wants. Over the years, I've encountered two types of people. The first are those who want God to be happy with what they do, and the second are those who want to do what makes God happy. Jesus said it like this: "The Father has not left Me alone, for I always do those things that please Him" (John 8:29). Did you know that Jesus was baptized solely to please God, His Father? Speaking to John the Baptist, Jesus said His baptism would "fulfill all righteousness," and afterward an approving voice from heaven affirmed, "This is My beloved Son, in whom I am well pleased" (Matt. 3:15, 17).

We Must Be More Interested in Heaven's Requirements Than in Earth's Accolades

Do you want to please God? If so, you must not only desire to please Him but believe you can and then commit to do so. However, take courage. Whenever you make the choice to obey God, He will reveal Himself and mentor you. When you choose to walk away from the world and walk toward God, He will meet you there. When you separate yourself from ungodly people, He draws closer to you. After I came to Christ, pleasing God was never something I felt like I had to do. To me, pleasing God was something that I had the incredible opportunity to do. I constantly reminded myself, *I can't live my life not doing all that I can to please Him. Pleasing God is everything I want.*

As you've probably already discovered, wanting to do what's right doesn't mean that you always do it, do you? When we intend to do what's right but choose to do otherwise, God usually won't hinder us. That is why we must die to self, take up our cross, and follow Christ (Matt. 16:24). Defeating self only happens when you and I are alone with God and His Word. It is at that place where you must face off with the side of you that desires to disobey and nail it to the cross and follow Him.

Years ago, any time Linda would leave the house, the devil would really bother me. He would taunt me, causing me to fear being alone. Please understand, I was a committed Christian at this time, but the devil would constantly harass me, spouting, *You wait until I get you alone. I'm going to let you have it. You'll never make it. I'm going to torment you. I'll destroy your life. You'll never become anything. I'll kill you. You think God can help you? Where's God right now? Why isn't He saying anything at this moment?* I was afraid and wondered how long I could face this torment every time Linda went away.

Fed up with being pushed around, I finally decided to deal with it head-on. One day I said to Linda, "Sweetheart, I want you to go away for the weekend." I stated emphatically to the devil, "I'm sending her away. When she leaves, you and I have an appointment. I'm tired of you pushing me around, making me afraid each time Linda goes anywhere."

When you challenge your fears, no one can go with you; you must go alone. David said, "Though I walk through the valley of the shadow of death, I will fear no evil" (Ps. 23:4). Aware that I had to face the devil, I needed to prove to myself, before all of heaven, that he really was a defeated liar! So no sooner did Linda leave than I began to confront the devil. I began to tackle the fears and worries that had me so tightly bound. Instead of running away, I began running to search for my "adversary the devil [who] walks about like a roaring lion, seeking whom he may devour" (1 Pet. 5:8).

You may be thinking, *do people need to do that?* There are times when I do believe people need to meet the enemy head-on. You can handle life any way you want to, but if you know the enemy is pursuing, don't run. Instead, stand up and fight! While alone, I confronted all the internal issues I was experiencing, making sure to fight each of them until I knew that I had defeated every last one. By the time that weekend was over, the devil couldn't lie to me any longer. The torment and the fear of being alone had utterly vanished.

I was victorious over the devil that day, but truthfully, this fight is not difficult to win; it's just difficult to make the decision to fight. How did I overcome? I overcame by taking the lies the enemy was telling me, bringing them directly before God and His Word, allowing Him to mentor my mind. Every time the devil lied to me, I would reply, "You tell God what you just told me!" Subsequently, there was a stony silence. As I proceeded to do that with each negative thought, those thoughts soon began to disappear. But it was only through the hidden power of being alone with God, having Him mentor my mind through His Word, that led me to confront the enemy and win.

In solitary moments, how can you use the Word of God to refine yourself into a person who pleases Him? Here are a few ways to get started.

1. Refuse to believe that you are the only one who is having trouble with your mind.
2. Identify the negative thoughts that consistently and presently bombard your mind.
3. Find a scripture to replace those thoughts and meditate on each one throughout the day, realizing that you can't just stop thinking about something; you must replace negative thoughts with God's Word.
4. Take the scripture and turn it into a positive confession, speaking it every day as often as possible.

Once you make the decision to fight when you're alone, you will always come out on top. Please realize that my motivation to fight the devil was not to be free in and of itself. No, my sole desire was to please my Father.

I fight for freedom because God is all I want. God is all I have. I fight for freedom because I refuse to believe the lie that the devil is stronger in my life than God. I have graduated from focusing on what I get out of this life into a school that teaches me to consistently pursue what is right for someone else. No longer am I interested in what *I* can get, but I'm more interested in what I can give God.

In hushed solitude came the discovery of how greatly I desired God. Did I really want to please Him? How much did I want God to transform me? I decided I wanted to please God enough to allow His Word to mentor my mind. And as He alters and mentors my mind, the manner in which I treat others has likewise been altered—the love and affirmation received from spending time alone with God compels me to extend the equivalent to every individual I meet.

—⚬—

In the book of Proverbs, while alone with God, Israel's King Solomon created the greatest wisdom in the world. In Ecclesiastes, alone with God, this same king realized that everything in this world is pure vanity. And in the Song of Solomon, alone with God, a beautiful allegory emerged, comparing man's relationship with God to that of the marital union.

chapter nine

PRISTINE PERSPECTIVE

Hurricane Katrina forever changed the direction of countless thousands of lives, didn't it? Well, just as a hurricane possesses the ability to change the force of the sea, when alone with God, His power has the ability to change the force, direction, and flow of our lives for decades to come. Not only does God's power change us as individuals, but it transforms us into vessels God can use to touch His people. We must allow His power to work in our lives not only so we can be blessed but so we can be a blessing to others.

When you utilize the moments you have alone by taking God's Word and renewing your mind, you then become the person to whom God can reveal His heart. God's power changes how you feel about your spouse, your kids, about your life as a whole. His power changes you completely. No longer will you view a person from a human perspective, but the Bible says you begin to see them from God's purely pristine perspective (2 Cor. 5:16). That means everyone, including yourself. No longer should you consider yourself as who you *were*; instead, regard yourself as who you *are* in Christ Jesus. Remember, Jesus sees us as a new creation, and that's how we must regard ourselves. "Your old life is dead. Your new life, which is your real life—even though invisible to spectators—is with Christ in God. He is your life" (Col. 3:3 MSG).

Allow this stirring account to encourage you:

Prior to being saved I led a completely heathen life with Halloween being my favorite holiday. I was a *very* heavy drug and alcohol user who left home at thirteen, in a rebellion that started after being sexually abused. I was crude and mean to everyone around me. After a horrible adult life, I ended up bedridden for six weeks before I finally had back surgery. While I was laid up in bed, I was weaned from the illegal drugs and alcohol, but I was loaded with all kinds of prescription drugs. While I lay there, I decided that I needed to change my life. I started to cry out to God out loud. I never wondered if He existed or could hear me; I just believed He could.

After I recovered, I ended up leaving the company where I had been working. On my way to resign, I looked up through my sunroof and asked God to help me handle myself properly with the owner. The meeting went extremely well, and I left the company in peace. As I exited the building, I looked up to the sky again and told God that now I needed a job. Before this meeting, I had applied at other places with no response, even though I hadn't been jobless since I was thirteen.

When I arrived home, the phone was ringing. The caller was a former coworker wondering if I knew anybody for a job opening at another company. The employer was more than excited that I was available and hired me the next morning. While I was employed there, my boss led me to the Lord and invited me to church. I was very excited to hear the teaching and felt like there was suddenly some direction in my life. I continued to come every week, bringing my daughter. We loved it! We would come home from service more joyous than we had ever been. My husband noticed this right away and started wondering what was going on with us.

As soon as we heard about it, my nine-year-old daughter and I attended a class about the foundational things of Christ. The teaching transformed my time reading the Bible into a time that built my relationship with Jesus. A friend of the family helped me choose an *NIV Application Bible*. God changed my life with this Bible! I had tried to read the Bible other times in my life and never could understand it. I was completely excited and so hungry to find out everything that Bible had to teach me.

Every morning for over four years, I'd wake up by 4 a.m. energized to read more and hear from God. There were times when I'd be in His presence for four hours that felt like ten minutes. My boss kept inviting me to a believers' gathering called a life group. My daughter and I didn't have a clue what to expect, but we haven't missed a church service or life group since unless we were on vacation or delivering a baby in the past five years.

I would often call two strong believers I had met at life group, sometimes daily, about questions I had about things I was learning in the church services or in my time alone with God. They were always very excited to help me understand and grow. It is because of their example and instruction that our roots have grown down so deep. There is not any storm that could uproot us at this point in our walk. Through God's changes in me, my husband now walks with God and has taken his position as leader in our household and of our life group.

God has promoted us so much now that people of our past hardly recognize us anymore. Our old selves have died, and we are definitely new people in Christ.

By enduring the process of transformation, this woman and her entire family was dramatically changed. Over the years, I've witnessed numerous people who are unwilling to endure the process of transformation. Instead of hanging in there long enough to see a change, they are always hunting down an instantaneous miracle. People make the grand mistake of identifying with their past yet neglecting to fully embrace their new identity in Christ.

The old Robb Thompson was unplugged on October 28, 1975. I was unplugged and reengineered and then plugged in again to Christ. As Ephesians 5:8 describes, "You were once darkness, but now you are light in the Lord."

Can you visualize a light within a human being turned down so low that the light that emanated from within was utter darkness? In your home, you may have dimmers on your light switches. You can actually lower the lights so much that the room is barely lit; even with the light on, the room is still dark. The light that once shone from you was utterly dark, but now God has reengineered you and has given you the power so that you can plug back into Life Himself. You are now the light of the world, the city that's set on a hill that cannot be hidden. But you must access the power of God and His Word in order to totally change.

The person God uses lives as Paul did, with a sense of purpose, saying, "I've got my eye on the goal, where God is beckoning us onward—to Jesus. I'm off and running, and I'm not turning back" (Phil. 3:13–14 MSG). This person attunes his mind to God's way of thinking. He obeys God's scriptural directives, such as "keep on," "continue," "eagerly pursue," "cultivate," "become progressively," and "constantly," as well as "advancing steadily," "increasing in the knowledge of God," "being continually built up in Him," and "keeping spiritually fit."

Historically, great armies of this world have overtaken strategic towns, cities, and nations, holding on to them as mighty strongholds. Over time we develop thought patterns that become personal strongholds. These strongholds become a part of our subconscious mind—causing us to operate from habit and no longer conscious choice. These habits shape our personalities, and we begin to think and act accordingly. *That's just the way I am*, we tend to think. People who know us describe us as "Oh, that's Fred. He's just an angry person," or "There's Susan, down-in-the-mouth as usual."

DON'T LET YOUR PAST DETERMINE YOUR FUTURE

The number one predictor of future behavior is past behavior. Statistics convey that 80 percent of people who molest a child will commit the act repeatedly. You can catch them, but catching them doesn't change the behavior of eight out of ten of them; they just replicate their destructive behavior all over again. But with the Word of God, we can renew our minds and thus change the dominant pictures inside our minds. Our minds, you see, constantly take photographic memories of people's behavior—good or bad. And as our mind's eye constantly scans those pictures, we tend to identify with the behavior, ultimately proceeding down the prescribed path.

Instead of mimicking those with whom we are in daily contact, Jesus advised us to deny ourselves, take up our cross, and follow Him. We do this by looking intently into the perfect law of liberty, the Holy Scriptures. Over a period of time we can actually reprogram our minds to think the way God thinks, identifying and imitating His holy behavior.

And how *did* Jesus behave? He would purposely separate Himself from the crowd in order to spend time with God. Luke 5:16 tells us that Jesus "often withdrew into the wilderness and prayed." Jesus withdrew, and when He did, He made the most of it! *Alone was where Jesus connected with God.* Alone was where Jesus built and fortified His life's foundation so that even in a crowd, He stayed connected to His vertical relationship with God. Undistracted by the taxing voices of the multitudes surrounding Him, He always made His Father top priority. As so must we. Surrendering to God's Word only happens when we decide to become alone internally, as Jesus did, with the expectation that we will connect with God amid the chaos that often besieges us.

After you surrender to God, everything in your life centers on your decision to be transformed by the renewing of your mind. The question remains: will you embrace God's thoughts or stubbornly cling to your own? Only you can answer that! Refuse to allow the status quo to mold your personality, your priorities, and your direction in life. Allow God to forge your character through moments alone with His Word.

STOP BEING A MIMIC AND START BEING A VOICE

The day must come when you stop imitating the voices around you and start being your own voice for following God. Here is how one woman did it:

In November 1994, I was desperately seeking a real God. You see, earlier that year my husband did something that devastated me. It wasn't really all about what he did at that moment, but it was just that everything hit me all at once—all of the abuse from my childhood, the neglect, the rejection from my mother and the abandonment of my dad, the drugs, the alcohol, the rape, and the abusive marriage I was now in.

I took my two girls and put them in the back seat of the car and began to drive. I had a habit of trying to run from things, but now I didn't want to run anymore. I was tired of running. I really just wanted to die. While driving in my car, I was crying so hard I could barely see the road. I knew there was nowhere to go; there was no one to turn to. I was coming up on a curve in the road, and I had a thought that I was going to pick up my speed as fast as I could and just let go of the steering wheel.

Obviously I wasn't in my right mind. Anything could have happened to me and the girls. But as I was approaching the curve and picking up speed, I began hitting the steering wheel and yelling to God, "If You're real, I need You to do something right now because I'm about to take my life and my little girls' lives."

In that moment, something happened unlike anything I'd ever known. At the time, I didn't know what it was, but now I know that it was the presence of God. A peace like I'd never known before came over us. I felt like rolling down the windows, and when I did, I felt as though darkness left us. All of a sudden, joy came over me. When I looked in the back at my girls, who had been crying just a moment earlier, I saw them laughing; so I knew it wasn't just me that this presence was hitting. I felt like God was speaking to me, and He was telling me that it was going to be all right.

This experience started my journey to find a church. I asked God to give me a sign when I walked into the right one. The only thing I knew He could show me was that presence, that peace that came over me in the car. I started going into all kinds of churches; I'd walk in and walk right back out. Finally, almost a year later, I walked into a church and felt that presence come over me. I heard God say that this was where I belonged.

The Bible teachings influenced my life so much. I began to spend time alone with God in His Word. I pored through Scriptures, meditating on them, speaking them day and night; it was the only time I could have peace in my mind. As I meditated on these Scriptures, I began to fight to be freed from alcohol, drugs, depression, and fear. I knew I didn't want them anymore, but they had been a part of my life for so long!

When I let them go and replaced that feeling for them with the Word of God, I got further and further away from that lifestyle. My life actually began to be transformed by renewing my mind with the Word of God. The Word of God has been the only truth that has set me free.

My time alone with the Word of God has freed me from many things: drugs and alcohol, depression, fear, mental illness, and suicidal thoughts. But more than anything, and this is what is most important to me, my children were freed from not having to live the life I grew up in.

My time alone with God and renewing of my mind on a daily basis is still to this day the most important thing in my life. Without it, I would be destroyed.

Because this woman allowed God's Word to transform her, she was liberated from her prison of destructive habits and secured a better life for herself and her family.

MAKE GOD'S WORD THE BASIS FOR YOUR THOUGHTS

Less than 10 percent of the people I know keep God at the center of their thoughts. How can I say that? I say that because although they are nicely dressed, wear a nice smile, and speak nice words, and although I may love them, their behavior proves otherwise—they have yet to be transformed by God's Word.

In moments when you are alone, I encourage you to ask the Lord to search your heart and try your thoughts (Ps. 139:23–24). As He reveals the not-so-pretty intentions within you, humbly bow and repent and relentlessly meditate on the Word of God.

It is important for all of us to learn this lesson: in order to transform your life, you must first be willing to change your mind. When you change your mind, your life will change. When your life changes, you draw closer to those who are drawing closer to God.

Take a moment and ask yourself the following thought-provoking questions:

- *What ungodly habits have I created in my life?* If you constantly worry, then when alone with God, you should constantly deposit into your mind the seed of Philippians 4:7: "And the peace of God, which transcends all understanding, will guard your hearts and your minds in Christ Jesus" (NIV). Create a thought-transforming confession that agrees with this verse, such as: "The peace of God guards my heart and mind in Christ Jesus." Repeat it until you believe it. It is only that which you believe that you do. Many people know God's Word, but they don't believe it fully and therefore they act according to their emotions and circumstances.

- *Do I habitually yell at my kids?* Meditate on this passage: "But the fruit of the Spirit is love, joy, peace, patience, kindness, goodness, faithfulness, gentleness and self-control" (Gal. 5:22–23 NIV).

- *Do I habitually criticize my spouse?* Then meditate on this scripture: "Watch the way you talk. Let nothing foul or dirty come out of your mouth. Say only what helps, each word a gift" (Eph. 4:29 MSG).

- *Do I habitually slander my mother-in-law?* Meditate on these words: "Bear with each other and forgive whatever grievances you may have against one another. Forgive as the Lord forgave you" (Col. 3:13 NIV).

- *Do I hold resentment against someone I work with?* Focus on this: "Rid yourselves of bad feelings toward others . . . putting on behavior marked by kind feeling" (Col. 3:8, 12 AMP).

- *Am I ungrateful?* "Cultivate thankfulness" (Col. 3:15 MSG).

- *When someone pulls in front of you in traffic, does "@*!!" habitually flow through my mind?* Because the Word commands "you must rid yourselves of . . . filthy language" (Col. 3:8 NIV), you can confess Ephesians 4:29: "I watch the way I talk. I let nothing foul or dirty come out of my mouth. I say only what helps, each word a gift" (MSG).

As you meditate on God's Word, it will soon change your pattern of thinking and your way of acting. The Word of God is so much more than static words on a page. It is active and alive! Meditating on God's Word is something you can do throughout the entire day—you don't need to be alone physically, but by being alone with your thoughts you are constantly reminded of what God says. I know some people who set their watches or cell phone alarms to periodically remind themselves to ponder a verse. Listen to this woman's story:

By meditating on and confessing scriptures day and night, my thoughts have completely changed. Before, I would allow myself to think about things that I shouldn't have. I now know that I don't have to accept those thoughts, so I exchange them for God's thoughts. By keeping scriptures constantly in front of me and on my lips, I'm always thinking God's thoughts. I don't want any thoughts but His.

Instead of aimlessly agreeing with every idle thought that enters your mind, you can utilize moments alone to direct your thoughts to please God and glorify Him, and His pristine perspective will soon belong to you.

—⚋—

In Isaiah 6, alone with God, the prophet Isaiah was awarded a spectacular view of heaven; while in Jeremiah 1, alone with God, the prophet's mouth was touched by the Lord's hand. And in Lamentations, alone with God, this same prophet wept and pleaded for the restoration of an entire nation.

chapter ten

REVIVED RECEIVERS

Whether it was Moses, seemingly cornered on the shore of the Red Sea, Queen Esther's perilous decision to entreat the king concerning the Jews, or Daniel's long night in the lions' den, what is often deemed as the worst of times frequently generates the best of times, times in which we are wonderfully and spectacularly revived.

For me, it was the best of times, but it was also the worst of times.

It appeared to be the cause of my craziness, but it was the only thing that gave me the strength to live.

I feared it more than anything, yet it has become a place of comfort.

It almost destroyed my life, yet it has been the only thing that really ever built me up. So tormenting, yet teaching me so much.

What on earth am I talking about? I am referring to the times I have been alone, both then and now.

For so many people, this alone time may be as rare as a desert rain. But as we search for more time alone and finally find it, for the most part we are clueless as to what to do with it. Being alone is often the moment when fear comes alive, but it is also the moment when you not only confront those fears, but like Moses, Esther, and Daniel, you conquer them as well.

My testimony isn't so much about the one-time miraculous salvation experience, but is more about how God can transform a young man who was once mentally bound. Beginning with my initial encounter alone with Him as a six-year-old boy, transformation occurred when I was able to break away and get alone with God. Without time alone, I would not be where I am at today. Once I was willing to face my fears and embrace God's Word, He began and has continued to accomplish a great work in my life.

Everyone experiences a transformation journey, no matter how dramatic or routine. One gentleman describes his journey this way:

After I became born-again, my relationship with God started with just reading His Word. Nothing else really mattered to me as I was intrigued by the new journey that I was about to take. I started with a modern translation of the New Testament. I quickly saw the need for some regimentation, so I began using daily devotionals. Initially, there was no need to motivate myself as the thirst I had for the Bible was insatiable. Then I learned the benefits of confessing it, listening to it, and meditating on it.

Godly men throughout history, such as Tertullian, Athanasius,

Augustine of Hippo, Thomas Aquinas, John Wycliffe, Martin Luther, John Newton, and Dietrich Bonhoeffer, have captured and enjoyed extraordinarily monumental moments while being alone with God. In his sermon "Walking with God," eighteenth-century British evangelist George Whitefield advised, "Be frequent . . . in meditation, all ye that desire to keep up and maintain a close and uniform walk with the most high God."

In his "Preface to Standard Sermons," famed English preacher John Wesley aptly relayed:

Here then I am, far from the busy ways of men. I sit down alone; only God is here. In His presence I open, I read His Book; for this end, to find the way to heaven. Is there a doubt concerning the meaning of what I read? Does anything appear dark or intricate? I lift up my heart to the Father of lights. Lord, is it not thy Word, "If any man lack wisdom, let him ask of God"? Thou "givest liberally and upbraidest not." Thou hast said, "If any be willing to do thy will, he shall know." I am willing to do, let me know thy will. I then search after and consider parallel passages of Scripture, "comparing spiritual things with spiritual." I meditate thereon, with all the attention and earnestness of which my mind is capable. If any doubt still remains, I consult those who are experienced in the things of God, and then the writings whereby, being dead, they yet speak. And what I thus learn, that I teach.

Perhaps you might relate to the following account:

I went through a time of discouragement and not wanting to take the time to spend alone-time with God. I think it was because, as we do so many times, I allowed my ideas of what it should be like to influence me. There would be times when I would sit there and couldn't feel a tangible presence of God, so I felt like He was probably at someone else's alone-time at that moment. I didn't hear His voice speak to me. It happened on more than one occasion for a while.

One day when I wasn't in that designated time with Him, I heard Him say to me that in my expectation of what our time should be like, I had started to treat Him and put Him in the same category as people treat each other. He said that I was feeling as though He didn't view me as important as He viewed someone else. He reminded me that He didn't love me any less than anyone else. He reminded me that He couldn't lie, and He told me that He would never leave or forsake me. He reminded me that if I invited Him in, He would come. When I go into my designated time with God now, I know that He is always there to meet me. Sometimes I don't feel prompted to even say anything. I'll just sit quietly, reassured that His presence is with me and will always be with me.

Shut Down Your Transmitters and Turn Up Your Receivers

So what does effective time alone with God look like? Many people picture a perfect environment where low music or Scriptures resonate in the background, an environment where they must allow themselves to sink into a semi-catatonic state where they can begin to feel the presence of eternity washing over their souls. But that is not the case at all! People think they must search for a place to spend moments alone—and I agree with that. But I have also made a surprising discovery. Your time alone with God is the moment you shut down your transmitters and turn up your receivers.

Monks are best at being in a crowd while simultaneously remaining in tune with their meditation. You, too, can be alone with God in a crowd, or wherever you choose. Each and every moment, you and I are either communicating vertically or horizontally. While at work, visiting a shopping mall, maneuvering your car, or drenched beneath your shower at home, you can commune with God.

Are you aware that a harried mother of four lively kids, driving to after-school activities in the family van, can still be alone with God? Let's say this lovely lady drives her children all over town to their piano lessons and athletic practices. Without warning, she abruptly finds herself reflecting about life. If she habitually is overwhelmed, she should ask herself, *what am I thinking about?* She may discover that her predominant thought is, *I'll never be able to get everything done.* So the question remains, will she revive her receivers enough by allowing God to transform her thoughts so that she doesn't live in a constant state of worry, or will she continue down the path of anxiety and stress?

One effective way of allowing God to transform her thoughts is by taking a few key passages and pondering them throughout her day. As she does so, her mind will begin to change. And as her mind changes, her life will steadily improve.

People often ask me, "How much do you pray every day?" I think a moment and respond, "Now that I think about it, I never stopped."

Do you need to break away and spend time reading the Scriptures? Yes, you do.

Do you need to have a time of prayer and solitude? Yes, you do.

Do you need to have a time where you confess the Word of God? Yes, you do.

But don't let it stop there. Allow it to become a lifestyle. Why not strive to cultivate a *lifestyle* of prayer, confessing God's Word and trusting Him during every situation of your day? That is why the Bible instructs us to "pray without ceasing" (1 Thess. 5:17).

Time with God isn't confined to a geographical location. But at the same time, your most intimate times with God won't happen in a crowd.

Just as time alone with your spouse is the key to intimacy in your marriage, time alone with God is one of the keys to intimacy with God. Remember, spending time alone with God is essentially about relationship. Jesus didn't escape the crowd because He *had* to pray. No, Jesus tore Himself away from the throng because He yearned to spend time with His Father. As a marriage won't thrive unless a husband and a wife focus on each other, neither will a relationship with God thrive unless we make spending time alone with Him our top priority.

Spend Private Time with God

Your most intimate and life-changing moments will occur when you spend private time with God. Here is one woman's description of her time alone with God. It powerfully illustrates intimate moments with the Lord:

> Recently widowed, I've had more time on my hands. I no longer need to see after my husband or our six children, who are now grown and gone from my home.
>
> I have created a "secret place" in my bedroom where I can arise early to dance and sing in my wonderful Savior's ear at least two songs. It reminds me that God really is my maker and husband.

I feel cherished and aglow with His presence. I then read my daily excerpt from a wisdom book and journal my "faith in action" goals according to the verse of the day. I resolve to commit the verse to memory that day and often succeed.

I then do my daily preparation for work—dressing and hygiene—while praying in tongues and continuing to listen to music. As I look in the mirror, I speak to myself in confession of the Word.

I then proceed out of my bedroom to the kitchen, where I have a fresh mental attitude with which to face my work as a home-health hospice nurse. I often have twenty-five to thirty voice messages to wade through. Previously I have allowed myself to become upset and fretful at the incompetence of others (which often comes to light as I receive repeat messages). Now I use it as an opportunity to pray for my supervisors and coworkers in a humble attitude. I never want to move away from my daily dance partner during the day by getting offended.

Usually, during my day I have opportunity to pray with or for my patients, which is a golden opportunity for putting their hands in God's hand. I know that when I don't see them as my assignments, I tend to become distracted by their physical and emotional needs, never getting to their spiritual needs at all. I've repented for enough missed opportunities through my own self-centeredness to finally realize that I want to please God instead of others and myself. Spending time with God between appointments in the car is a splendid time to confer with Him about the patient I've just left and also the one I'm about to see. God is interested in every aspect of my day, and I want to stay in step with Him during the dance.

I stop at a track almost daily for a four-mile power walk when I can pray in tongues and with the understanding for others. Resisting distractions is a major problem by this time of day. I repeatedly need to ask the Spirit's help to press into the prayer needs of the day. My mind seems so cluttered by late afternoon and prefers to daydream or focus on mundane events, people, or things. I frequently find it necessary to bind the enemy and loose obedience so I can pray heartfelt, focused prayers and be a good steward of God's time.

At bedtime I read the Psalms, particularly Psalm 119, and write insights next to the verses. I say good night to my dance partner and sleep. All is well with my soul!

In her message entitled "12 Ways to Defeat the Devil," Joyce Meyer exhorts, "The only way that we're going to stay strong is to spend good, regular, personal, quality time with God."[1]

When you decide to spend time alone with God, He sees your heart along with your desire to know Him intimately. And He has plans to reward you for your diligent pursuit. But we must turn up our revived receivers and get alone with Him.

—∞—

In Ezekiel 1, alone with God, the priest Ezekiel witnessed the heavens open and viewed exciting visions from God; while in Daniel 2, alone with God, the interpretation of King Nebuchadnezzar's baffling dream was ultimately disclosed. In Hosea 1, alone with God, Hosea was astoundingly charged to marry a prostitute as a vivid portrayal of Israel's harlotry toward God; while in Joel 2, alone with God, a great prophecy of the Holy Spirit was given.

chapter eleven

DESTRUCTIVE DISTRACTIONS

Fifteen minutes before another workday begins, a half hour following dinner, or a few quiet moments before climbing into bed—slowing down long enough to schedule blocks of time alone is a complex hurdle for just about all of us. To summarize Isaac Newton's first law of motion, a body's natural tendency is to maintain its state of motion. Therefore, when we are at rest, we tend to stay at rest; and when we are running around trying to accomplish things, we tend to stay in motion.

Many people are reluctant to spend time alone with God because they remember how dry the Word was the last few times they read it. Others may balk because they recall a past inability to feel God's presence. Disheartened before they even begin, many speculate, *is it really worth the time?* No wonder that being alone with God often becomes a ritualistic duty, another thing to check off our to-do list rather than a pleasure to be anticipated. Anything done in duty soon becomes drudgery.

We live in an age where there's so much to accomplish yet so little time in which to accomplish it, don't we? Many people feel overwhelmed because there doesn't seem to be enough hours in the day to do everything on their to-do list. So when hearing that they need to spend more time with God, they see no way of that ever being a possibility. They throw up their hands and exclaim, "Just another thing that won't get done." You may be that person. If so, I understand exactly how you feel, and I am certain as you continue to read you'll discover how people just like you found time to spend with God while getting done all they needed to get done and more.

In recent years, women have identified time pressure as a major issue in their lives. Disillusioned with "having it all," many women concur with the lyrics of Amy Grant's song "Hats": "This may be a dream come true, but when it all comes down it's an awful lot to do."[1]

And men can relate to the Beatles' lyrics: "It's been a hard day's night, I should be sleeping like a log."[2] But when men return home from the office needing rest and relaxation, do they get it? Not often enough. The minute they walk through the door they face the sincere requests of their spouse: "Honey, can you get the kids to come to the dinner table? Oh, and after dinner we have to talk; I couldn't pay all the bills."

Women say they need time alone to regroup, rejuvenate, refresh, refocus, relax, read their Bible, work out, and work on the goals they set for themselves. And if they don't get it, they feel as though the wheels start falling off the wagon of their lives. Author Susan Taylor describes it this way: "We need quiet time to examine our lives openly and honestly. . . . Spending quiet time alone gives your mind an opportunity to renew itself and create order."[3] It allows you to connect with God in a way that life normally doesn't allow us to do.

One woman who works full time outside her home says,

I highly rate my time alone because I really enjoy being by myself. I realize that this is probably because I don't often have alone-time. Constantly interacting with people at work and at home makes time alone difficult to find. Yet on the flip side, if I am by myself for too long, I have to get around people; otherwise I would go crazy!

Another working mother describes her life like this:

Working a full-time job filled with helping people, I must say that right now I desire more alone-time. I think if I were a stay-at-home mom or spent my days working alone, I would desire more time with people. I'm appreciative of the people I get to work with on a daily basis; however, when it's time to leave the office, I'm grateful.

Although men tend to worry about accomplishing their goals, it seems as though women are more prone to stress about unaccomplished daily tasks. Many Christian women today highly value time alone, but most lament not finding enough of it. And when they're finally able to find some, they tend to preoccupy it with busyness. For most, that means catching up—doing piles of laundry, dealing with endless pieces of mail, and nonstop cleaning.

Here is how one woman puts it:

I tend to feel overwhelmed because my to-do list is always longer than the amount of time I have to accomplish it. My tendency is to worry about how I will get everything done, to get depressed because things are not as neat as I would like, and to feel guilty for being tired or taking a nap when there is so much that needs to get done.

Another woman describes how hard it is to find time alone for herself and for God in her current situation:

When can I squeeze in some alone-time? I don't know how to be alone, because my mind lives on a to-do list, or a what-not-to-forget list. I definitely desire more time alone since I work full time, have a husband, a one-year-old, a four-year-old, a small business, and am highly active at church. I just need enough time alone where I can get on the computer to keep up with our paperwork, the business paperwork, and housework without my little guys either hanging on me or just needing me. Although I wouldn't trade my life for anything, more time is something I would love to have to get things done in just a little more timely and efficient manner.

In order to spend some time alone with God, I get up around 3 or 4 a.m. at least three times a week just to pray for a while in our worship room. Truthfully, this way it's too dark to clean the house, and my kids and husband are asleep so I can give God undivided attention.

Whether male or female, I'm sure you can relate. So how *can* you use time alone more wisely and efficiently? Listen to what one individual wisely observed: "A lot of times, you feel like you are going, going, going in order to get more things done, but I believe that if I could build in more alone times with God, then I could get more done in less time."

Another woman combats thoughts of guilt and worry about her inability to get everything done by "continuing to look to God's ability instead of my inability. I practice casting my care and rejoicing instead of worrying, and choosing gratitude over depression. As long as I am confessing the Word and feeding my faith, I am doing fine and winning this battle. It is a choice. Most important, I try to laugh as much as possible and not take myself too seriously."

It never ceases to amaze me how when people finally do get alone with their thoughts, if they are honest, they'd admit they do anything they can to distract themselves so they don't feel the pain of their recent failures or past disappointments. Most resort to watching TV, surfing the Web, or talking on the phone. Despite fears and insecurities, there are others who do get alone to sit down and think, focusing on what they can change about themselves, not on what they can't. But they, too, would frequently admit a distaste of being alone with their thoughts. It's not necessarily enjoyable to begin this journey of being alone and facing your fears and anxieties, but unless we take the first step, we'll be bound toward the negative thoughts that constantly plague our minds.

On the other side of the coin, we should take a good look at our lives and admit that we have more time than we think, and perhaps we've developed some destructive habits. Poor time management has led to much busyness and needless stress. The moment we realize that our spouse and kids will be gone for a while, where is the first place we run? Do we seize the moment to interact with God, or do we rush to pay the bills, call a friend, or turn on the television?

What Do You Do When You Have Some Time Alone?

What is the first thing you do when you have some time alone? Ask yourself, *have I taken time to be with God today?* If not, then make the commitment to use the time you do have alone to pray and meditate on His Word. Frankly, when we take a closer look, we would all admit that we really do have time to give to God. We live in a culture where we enjoy more excess time and more discretionary money to entertain ourselves and divert our attention from God than ever before. But how destructive these distractions have become! The pleasures of life have diluted our desire for God and for seeking the things of God. Think for a moment: most people can spend up to two hours enjoying a movie but can hardly spend half an hour in prayer. If we're honest, we'll admit this is true even to ourselves.

Neglecting time with God only makes the thought of being alone with Him more painful. But being alone doesn't have to be a negative experience for any of us. I have decided that I won't allow my weaknesses to stop me from spending time alone with God. I yearn for Him to deal with me and help me overcome my fears and flaws. It takes a committed decision to spend time alone with God, and in the following story, this woman did just that:

> When I found myself living alone after divorce and with no money (having left my career due to early retirement), wondering where prosperity had fled to and struggling to find emotional healing, I finally decided to accept the challenge of creating a secret place for myself and waiting for the Holy Spirit to show up.
>
> I had to face my personal giants of rejection, fear of people,

and low self-esteem. I had to choose to believe that God's promises are true and not a lie, because I didn't see them happening as I expected them to. My only choice was to press in deeper, because nothing but failure waited in the other direction. Once I made that choice, the Holy Spirit was there to meet me.

I made a serious commitment to spend a significant amount of time with God first thing every morning. It didn't take very long before I was spending about two hours each day. Once in a while, it could go to four hours, and occasionally more than that. The Holy Spirit has been very gracious and kind to me, because He made His Presence known to me fairly quickly.

His Presence was so sweet that I didn't want to leave it. I began to grow much more quickly. I began to hear His voice. I determined in my heart to do what God wanted no matter what.

In my secret place, I had no rules; I just let Him lead, but two years in a row I disciplined myself to read through the Bible in a year, and I had my own list of confessions that I almost never missed. About two and a half years ago, I started taking personal Communion almost daily although I didn't let it become a ritual. I have had some amazing things happen just during Communion.

Lately I'm busier, but I still have daily morning quiet-time, usually with some Bible reading. I always do my confessions, and I always take Communion.

Those years when I had more time were foundational and built me up and brought me healing so that I am now stronger, wiser, more determined, and better able to serve God and love and serve others.

In my walk with God, I have learned to ignore thoughts that would lead to worry or fear. Thoughts come at us from every direction, and only those who are willing to ignore the negative thoughts will walk in true freedom.

WHAT ARE YOU WILLING TO IGNORE?

Your life is determined by what you're willing to ignore. Think about how Potiphar's wife lied about Joseph's character. Didn't he have to ignore the voice of offense? Prior to that, he had to disregard the voice of his brothers' rejection, and he had to additionally dismiss the voice of ridicule when he told them his dream. Consider this:

When Joseph's brothers threw him in the pit, Joseph was *alone*.

When Potiphar's wife tried to tempt him, in essence, Joseph walked *alone*.

When he was thrown in jail, Joseph was *alone*.

When he stood before Pharaoh, Joseph was *alone*.

When he saw his brothers once again, Joseph was *alone*.

Or *was* he? When God is the focus of your life, although situations may place you into an "alone circumstance," He is always there, right beside you. When you seek first *His* kingdom, He'll add to your life the very things that you need (Matt. 6:33).

You must ignore the voice that says, "You're not good enough." And you need to discount the voice that threatens, "You couldn't even get a man if you wanted one." From personal experience, I am well acquainted with the voice of failure that says, "Watch out! You better skip time with God and spend time with your kids instead or they'll turn out rotten."

Ask yourself, "Am I really the reason someone else fails?" Never allow the voice of failure to put the responsibility for someone else's success upon your shoulders. You were never meant to carry that load. You must take up and carry your own cross.

WHAT CHOICES ARE YOU MAKING?

The outcome of your life is determined by your choices. If you find yourself overwhelmed with destructive distractions, find encouragement in this family's story:

> After having my second child on October 3, 2003, I decided to go to school to get my degree as a certified medical assistant in January 2004. I have always wanted to be a nurse, and a program came up that allowed me to be at school from 5 a.m. to 9 a.m. and then be at my job that was around the corner from the school by 9:15. Work was still full-time (leaving at 5:15 p.m.), and my children were an hour away from work. Then it took an hour to get home, feed, shower, and hurry them into bed. For me, the night did not end once the children were in bed because I had to clean, wash laundry, shower, and do homework, all to begin again once I got up at 4 a.m. the next day.
>
> I finally finished school and worked in a wonderful doctor's office, but everything at home was falling apart. Our babysitter was no longer an option, and we had no choice but to put the children into day care. This was a wonderful place; however, the cost was equivalent to our monthly mortgage! We knew we needed to cut that cost. We had no time or money!
>
> Our schedule was so full. We both had full-time jobs, kids, busy church schedules, and family from both sides looking for visits, with no time to breathe! I felt like I gave God minutes on

and off within the day when I cried and begged for direction and guidance.

Then we started to think of options: I could stay at home with the house and kids full-time, or I could try working part-time and reducing day care costs.

I chose to try working only part-time, even though we knew the best option was to completely stop working. For my whole life, I had been trained to work. I liked physical work and loved working as a nurse, since I had always had a passion to be one. It was very hard to drop down to part-time work, but it was okay just as long as I still got to work.

Well, everything at home seemed to get worse. My oldest child was failing in school. My husband had to turn down work because he was at home with the kids (playing Mom) while I was at work during the evening. I was so tired, my church-serving schedule no longer worked out. My time with God was in the car rushing to work, washing dishes, or placing my head on my pillow at night.

I knew God could hear me crying out to Him, but I felt so distanced. I could feel the presence of God leaving my side, and that scared me more than the lack of money we were still experiencing. Every day I could feel myself crying inside for God and feeling like I was missing the best years of my children's lives.

Again, we started to talk about me staying at home full-time. Once I told my husband how I was feeling, our decision was almost made. I spoke with our district pastor and was encouraged.

I had been a mom for six years, but never a teacher, mentor, corrector, guide, or any of the other things that a mother placing her children into the hands of God would be, and this scared me.

Having a hard time going to work and starting to have the desire to be at home, we made the decision that I would finally come home. I had given my boss three weeks' notice to find another nurse. For three weeks they told me that I wouldn't leave because I was so passionate about my job, so they never found a replacement. I still decided to leave, and I came home and told my children.

My oldest cried and told me to go back and get my job. She did not understand that my original role was to be at home with her and not working. Her attitude eventually changed. It was hard coming home, and I had days when I cried. But God has so wonderfully placed us around great examples of families, and I feel continuously encouraged.

Now having the opportunity to seek God first, we have been able to change as a family and become strong in the Lord. We are able to pray together as a family and see the transformation that God has allowed in our lives. I am so grateful to God for the mercy He has shown us in this time of change.

After listening to this mother's story, what destructive distractions will you refuse? Replace those distractions and unnecessary curricular activities with alone-time with God because it is vital to your life.

In this way, transforming your minds to the Word of God is not about adding something to your schedule; it's something you add while going about your daily schedule. When it was my wife's turn to participate in a school carpool, she would pray over the children and have all of them confess the Word as she drove them to school, making sure they were ready for their day. Some mothers read Scriptures to their children as they eat their breakfast. Ask the Lord to show you what works best for your family. Any mother can fall into the trap of subconsciously elevating motherhood to an idolatrous level in her mind. Without realizing it, she can prioritize the perceived needs of her children above keeping God first in her life. Trying to accomplish all the things she thinks she must do to be a good mother, she can allow herself to become distracted from submitting to the Lord.

A single mother regularly needs to determine the most profitable paths for her children to follow. Many single moms decide to bring their children to church, and they are often the ones with obedient children. Some don't take time to teach them the Word of God because they say, "I need to give to them. I didn't give them a father, so now I need to make it up to them by giving them things they want." Everything she does is centered on her children, and those children degenerate into such self-centeredness that it takes a miracle to bring them out of it.

One of the things a single mother should realize is that her children will feel sorry for her because she doesn't have a man to ease her burdens. When they notice how much easier a woman's life is who has a man to help her, they become motivated to behave instead of becoming an extra burden. She needs to understand how to use that for their mutual benefit.

A wise thing she should do is set up a family schedule, remembering not to completely saturate it so that she can spend some time alone with God. She can tell her children the following: "On Sunday, we'll go to church together. On Wednesday, we'll attend the midweek service together. We will eat together; all other activities will fit around dinnertime. We're going to support each other's activities, but we're not going to be overly busy."

Setting this kind of family schedule allows her an opportunity for alone-time. It will also afford her the energy to support her children's outside interests. No matter how inadequately she feels concerning what her kids are missing, she cannot completely fill up her schedule, "for your Maker is your husband" (Isa. 54:5), and she knows better than to take time away from her "husband"—He needs her attention.

This woman also remembers the set time she has scheduled to devote to transforming her thoughts and attitudes to God's will. She knows, for instance, that from 7:00 to 7:30 a.m., she says certain confessions. She should ask herself, *am I able to read the Bible during my lunch hour?* She may pleasantly discover that she can read a few chapters every day at that time.

If you're a single mother, you can make a regimen so that when you get up in the morning, the most important thing you do is pray. First, pray for those in authority over you. Second, confess God's Word, which is another form of prayer. As a mother, you would want to make confessions from Scriptures such as Isaiah 54:13: "Great are my children's peace and their undisturbed composure. My children are taught of the Lord." And from Ephesians 1:17–18: "Thank You that You've granted my children a spirit of wisdom and revelation so that they can know You better. Thank You that the eyes of their understanding are enlightened so that they know the hope to which You have called them." All mothers who do this recognize that this time alone with God is nonnegotiable. And if you'll not break this nonnegotiable, God will honor you, for He honors those who honor Him.

One single mother describes her experience in learning how God is her heavenly husband:

I was a single mom for ten years with one growing son. At times I was working two or three jobs to support us as well as go to his ball games, be at church three times a week with him, and go to many school events. Many a vacation day was spent going on field trips with him and his classmates. Often I'd be overwhelmed with thoughts that I wasn't good enough to raise him and do all that I needed to do. Then I found Philippians 4:13: "Whatever I have, wherever I am, I can make it through anything in the One who makes me who I am" (MSG).

With God I was equipped and could be a good mom, employee, and fulfilled woman. It was when I left God out of the picture that my days were long and tiring. My alone-time with God was in the evenings after I put my son to bed. There were times I would fall asleep listening to God's voice, and this frustrated me. But one night I softly heard Him say to me, *As you read your son a story to quiet him and help him go off to sleep, so I do the same for you.*

I'll never forget how personal my God really was and how He was my husband and a father to my son during those years.

To spend quality time with God, what voices must you ignore? What specific time have you designated to seek God above all other priorities? He's worth it, and so are you. We must always remember that we're not creatures of discipline; we're creatures of habit. Therefore, we have to create habits. Habits will take you further than desire. Habits will take you a lot further than passion. To understand this, just observe the life of someone who is hooked on cocaine—his habit takes him further than his desire to be free.

Initially, changing and creating good habits may feel awkward, but I have realized that the height of human experience is not money, it's not marriage, it's not children, it's not success, and it's not enjoying this life. The height of the human experience is enjoying the presence of our Creator with the intent of bringing Him pleasure.

Consequently, I've found that one of the best ways to please the Father is to spend time with Him in solitary refinement, disregarding any destructive distractions that stand in the way.

—❧—

In Amos 9, alone with God, the shepherd Amos saw the Lord standing by the altar and heard Him speak! In Obadiah, alone with God, Obadiah was given a vision of the ancestors of modern-day Jews and Arabs. In Jonah 2, alone with God in the belly of the fish, Jonah acknowledged that salvation is of the Lord; and in Micah 1, alone with God, judgment against Samaria and Jerusalem was firmly unveiled.

chapter twelve

FABULOUS FUTURE

Children of all ages love to watch the spectacular feats of acrobatic aircraft. Skilled pilots can maneuver and invert these planes thirty feet off the ground, traveling at three hundred miles per hour. Don't you especially enjoy those chilling loop-the-loops? I think they're wonderful. But, when it's all said and done, it doesn't matter how much fun you had while in the air if the plane doesn't land correctly. If you crash, all those breathtaking memories of flying will be forgotten, won't they?

I think flying is a lot like life. In every situation and in every relationship, I live from the destination backward to my present circumstance. I ask myself, *Where do I desire to end up and where am I now? What must I do to get where I desire to go?* If I'm going see God face-to-face, if I'm going to be with Him for eternity, then how should I live today? As the apostle Peter advised, "No longer should [he] live the rest of his time in the flesh for the lusts of men, but for the will of God" (1 Pet. 4:2). Eighteenth-century theologian Jonathan Edwards determinedly resolved "never to do anything I'd be afraid to do, if it were the last hour of my life."

Failures do what gives them the present they desire. Successful people do what gives them the future they desire. The truth has no fanfare. The moment you discover truth, you also notice that its reality introduces you to a whole new array of things with which you must deal. Moments alone engage mental, emotional, and spiritual struggles—a time of wrestling and soul-searching regarding hidden issues and unresolved thoughts, pleading for us to formulate a decision. When we are alone, we confront things that lay hidden on the inside of us—intimate things we'd rather no one know about, things we are ashamed to admit openly, even to ourselves.

Due to my past sins and the assorted faults of my family, I have often felt as if I could not please God. Over the years, I have endured many of these thoughts and have been very hard on myself. From time to time, I could not believe I was repeatedly dealing with these same old relentless thoughts.

I finally made the decision to stop allowing negative thoughts to dictate who I was becoming. I began to see myself according to God's Word and not according to the negative thoughts that bombarded my mind. Never allow a poor view of yourself to dictate who God desires you to become. Refuse to permit your past to negatively determine the fabulous future God has planned. What I am in His eyes is who I really am. The more time I spend with Him, the less I focus on my low self-esteem. The closer I get to God, the more I embrace the sacrifice that made me clean.

By taking a quick glimpse at my family's routinely negative results, I can tell you how my life *should* have turned out. If the Word had not transformed me, I would be a failure through and through. One of my brothers died of hepatitis C. Another spends the majority of his time in jail. My family tree is populated with alcoholics and workings in the occult. How I thank God for His transforming power! When you break away from the busyness of life and spend a few moments with God, talking with Him and listening to His heart, you will receive some of the following life-changing benefits:

Benefit #1: Alone, You See God's Word More Clearly

God is not usually unearthed in the issues of life. No, the only time you really ever discover God's heart is when you purposely set those issues aside and listen to His Word. God is in the listening part of life. He's not in the earthquake, and He's not in the fire. His voice is contained in His Word. Through His Word, He is speaking continuously. The question I pose to you is, are you listening to what He is saying?

Luke 10:38–42 tells the story of Mary and Martha, two sisters who loved Jesus. Because they loved Him, Jesus wanted to visit their home and have a meal with them. When Jesus arrived, Mary left her sister, Martha, to prepare the food by herself. The longer Martha busied herself in the kitchen and the longer she noticed Mary sitting and talking to Jesus, the more exhausted and irritated Martha became. Martha became upset because Mary was doing what she wanted to do—recline at the feet of Jesus.

Some moments later, Martha complained, "Jesus, my sister, Mary, has left me alone to do all this serving." Gently, Jesus replied, "Now, Martha, you're bothered by a lot. You have a lot going on. There is much stress in your life." He continued, "But Mary has chosen what's right, and what she has chosen cannot be take away from her."

You see, there is a time to posture yourself as a listener—one who grows quiet before the Word of God. Mary *chose* to sit at the feet of Jesus. We should serve God's people, but we should never neglect time alone with God.

Do you remember the Western movies where the nervous gunman's itchy fingers squirmed restlessly on the trigger? Well, we must not be like those nervous gunmen. Living anxiously and impatiently will never get our prayers answered. We must quiet ourselves and get before His Word. Instead of living offended and angry with those who harmed you in the past, bow your knee to God's Word and walk in love. Allow God to heal your hurt, to make right their wrong. Accept God's love and cast your cares on Him, for He cares for you more than you'll ever know (1 Pet. 5:7). He cares about your struggles even more than you do. And best of all, He can handle them. You can't! So don't even try.

I am reminded of another biblical account in which a famine had plagued the land of Samaria, causing a hungry woman to desperately cry out to her king for help. When she saw him, she begged, "O king, please help me. Can you give me something to eat?" The king replied, "Ma'am, if the Lord cannot help you, I cannot help you" (2 Kings 6:25–27).

You see, God is our source, not America, nor our economy. God is our only source. David said it like this, "God is the strength of my heart and my portion forever" (Ps. 73:26). Trust me, if God cannot help you, then who can?

The purpose of prayer or time alone with God is not to change God but to change *us*. Understanding this gives a whole new perspective about time alone with God. Take a look at this woman's story:

I have a special place called the "Joy Path" where I love to go be alone with the Lord. Feeling overwhelmed when my kids were making bad choices, I decided one day to go for a walk on the Joy Path. As I walked, I took in the beauty and quiet, the sights and smells of the fragrant plants. I prayed quietly in the Spirit and laid down every burden upon the Lord.

My favorite tree in the world is along the Joy Path. I climbed the tree and waited, remembering how Jesus noticed Zacchaeus in a sycamore tree. As I stayed up in the tree, I felt the Lord ministering to me, giving me wisdom about how to handle the present situations.

I left and told my two errant teenagers that we were going on a field trip. I took them to the path and showed them the tree. They immediately climbed it just as I had done an hour before. As I joined them in the tree, I was able to correct them and they were able to receive it so easily that it was as if the Lord had anointed that place. They both repented of their actions and their bad attitudes. When we descended, we realized the Lord had given them a new, fresh start. It was a beautiful day!

BENEFIT #2: ALONE, YOU DISCOVER GOD'S HEART

The more time you spend alone with God, the more you'll discover His character, and the more you get to know His character, the more you will act like Him.

Over the years, I have been privileged to meet individuals I consider to be wonderful people. To this day, I chuckle when they say to me, "It's very difficult for me to understand how in the world your heart beats so close with God's." Does this happen automatically? No. It happens when God finds someone who desperately desires nothing more than to know and obey Him. When speaking to the prophet Samuel, God said, "I've searched the land and found this David, son of Jesse. He's a man whose heart beats to my heart, a man who will do what I tell him" (Acts 13:22 MSG).

Have you ever wondered why the Bible never talks about David's mother; it only identifies Jesse as David's father? When Samuel, the priest of Israel, invited Jesse to attend a sacrifice to the Lord, Jesse appeared with seven of his eight sons, excluding David. Because the Lord instructed Samuel to anoint one of Jesse's sons to be the next king of Israel, when Samuel saw the oldest son, he thought, *surely this is the one!* But the Lord advised Samuel not to observe the outward appearance, explaining that He looks at a person's heart (1 Sam. 16:7).

God said no to all seven sons, causing Samuel to ask Jesse if all of his sons were present. Jesse admitted that his youngest son was out tending the sheep, so Jesse sent for him. When David appeared, the Lord told Samuel, "Rise and anoint him; this is he" (1 Sam. 16:12 AMP).

God's Word shows us through this story that we should stop looking for acceptance from people—instead, seek the acceptance of God. People have this idea that God accepts everyone. Truthfully, He only accepts those who accept His Son's sacrifice. Once you bow your knee and repent, God welcomes you into His family. But even after being welcomed into His family, it is important to understand that the kingdom of God is not a democracy but a theocracy. Therefore, God's way of doing things must be maintained. And it is God alone who can satisfy you, who can make you happy, who can meet your every need.

If you're a husband, even if your wife expended every bit of energy and every bit of goodness she had to make you happy, she still could not satisfy your every need. That was not God's intention. He alone satisfies.

And if you think that you would be so much happier if you could just get a husband, you won't find complete satisfaction with him. On days when this wise woman's marriage isn't as easy as she hoped it would be, this is what she chooses to do:

> If I am dealing with a bad attitude because of unmet expectations, I know what the Word of God commands, so along with the scripture that states, "Love does not insist on its own way," I will picture how my response will be when my husband comes home. Just thinking of the scripture does not always help, as amazingly enough, the fangs come out at first sight of him. But if I picture myself acting out the verse—how I respond when he walks in and what I say—it is actually funny at times how well it works.

Most people trust anything and everything except God. They trust their business, their spouse, and even their money. Some erroneously dispute, "But God gave me my husband," or "God gave me this business," or "God gave me my kids." Never put your trust in anything except God alone. But in order to trust Him, you must seek Him diligently and get acquainted with His character and His Word.

The closer you walk with God, the more your hearts will beat as one.

BENEFIT #3: ALONE, YOU REFOCUS YOUR PRIORITIES

Ever have trouble keeping the big picture inside your mind? We're all tempted to place other things before our relationship with God, but we must look to Jesus as our example: "When Jesus perceived that they were about to come and . . . make Him king, He departed again to the mountain by Himself alone" (John 6:15).

Why did Jesus run from the potential moment of coronation? Rather than receive glory unto Himself, He refused to accept the praise and adoration of men. He cared only for the acceptance of His Father. Was Jesus interested in promoting Himself or being promoted by others? No, He simply chose to get alone. By being alone, He could silence the voices speaking against God's will and refocus His priorities and purpose.

And so can we, as this individual pleasantly discovered:

> I love time alone! It is a time to recoup from the pressures of living life, a time to get back in touch with the real me—the me who isn't trying to conform to the desires of another or to the mold of society. It is a time when I can reflect and meditate without any outside pressures.

BENEFIT #4: ALONE, YOU SEE AND EXPERIENCE GOD IN A FRESH WAY

For much of our lives, we hear about God and the things of God, and we learn about how God acts. Most people would boldly declare, "I know God" only to realize later in life that they knew *about* God but they didn't truly *know* God. Spending time alone with God is one of the keys to experiencing and seeing God in a fresh, new way.

Take a look at the life of the apostle Paul (formerly known as Saul) as he encountered God in a dramatic way:

> All this time Saul was breathing down the necks of the Master's disciples, out for the kill. He went to the Chief Priest and got arrest warrants to take to the meeting places in Damascus so that if he found anyone there belonging to the Way, whether men or women, he could arrest them and bring them to Jerusalem.
>
> He set off. When he got to the outskirts of Damascus, he was suddenly dazed by a blinding flash of light. As he fell to the ground, he heard a voice: "Saul, Saul, why are you out to get me?"
>
> He said, "Who are you, Master?"
>
> "I am Jesus, the One you're hunting down. I want you to get up and enter the city. In the city you'll be told what to do next."
>
> His companions stood there dumbstruck—they could hear the sound, but couldn't see anyone—while Saul, picking himself up off the ground, found himself stone-blind. They had to take him by the hand and lead him into Damascus. He continued blind for three days. He ate nothing, drank nothing. (Acts 9:1–9 MSG)

When the Lord instructed Ananias to help Saul,

> Ananias protested, "Master, you can't be serious. Everybody's talking about this man and the terrible things he's been doing, his reign of terror against your people in Jerusalem! And now he's shown up here with papers from the Chief Priest that give him license to do the same to us."

But the Master said, "Don't argue. Go! I have picked him as my personal representative to non-Jews and kings and Jews. And now I'm about to show him what he's in for—the hard suffering that goes with this job."

So Ananias went and found the house, placed his hands on blind Saul, and said, "Brother Saul, the Master sent me, the same Jesus you saw on your way here. He sent me so you could see again and be filled with the Holy Spirit." No sooner were the words out of his mouth than something like scales fell from Saul's eyes—he could see again! He got to his feet, was baptized, and sat down with them to a hearty meal. (Acts 9:13–19 MSG)

After this encounter, God changed Saul's name to Paul. Paul, of course, became one of the church's greatest apostles, enduring extensive persecution and personal suffering. Through an encounter alone with God, Saul experienced God in a fresh, new way—and so can we!

BENEFIT #5: ALONE, YOU FINALLY REALIZE YOUR DEPENDENCE ON GOD

After Moses died, God chose a young man named Joshua to be Moses' successor. Can you imagine how Joshua must have felt? Now he was absolutely alone. His mentor was no longer there to guide and lead him through the trying circumstances ahead. In desperation, Joshua had only one place to turn—God! God invited Joshua to step inside the sandals of a man who had spoken with Him face-to-face, as a man speaks to his friend (Ex. 33:11). The only other person in the Bible called "a friend of God" was the great patriarch, Abraham (James 2:23). Joshua, you see, was embarking on a responsibility far greater than himself. I'm sure he was fearful and uncertain if he could effectively handle the divine assignment. But as great as Moses was, he was unable to lead the children of Israel into the Promised Land, and now God was asking Joshua to do it!

Knowing the position Joshua was in, God encouraged him, saying, "Be strong and courageous, because you will lead these people to inherit the land I swore to their forefathers to give them. . . . Do not let this Book of the Law depart from your mouth; meditate on it day and night, so that you may be careful to do everything written in it. Then you will be prosperous and successful" (Josh. 1:6, 8 NIV). That day Joshua made the decision to completely depend on God and therefore was able to successfully lead the Israelites to the Promised Land.

Jeremiah was another man who was insecure and anxious. The prophet couldn't have fulfilled his destiny without depending on God. When God informed him, "I appointed you as a prophet to the nations," Jeremiah responded, "I do not know how to speak; I am only a child." God replied, "Do not say, 'I am only a child.' You must go to everyone I send you to and say whatever I command you. Do not be afraid of them, for I am with you and will rescue you" (Jer. 1:5–8 NIV). Alone is where Jeremiah, like Joshua, made the decision to listen and follow God.

God instructed another prophet, Jonah, to warn the city of Nineveh to repent for their wickedness. But Jonah had an issue: his pride got in the way. He wanted God to punish the Ninevites, who were enemies of Israel, rather than forgive them; so Jonah decided to flee. Instead of traveling to Nineveh, where God told him to go, he boarded a ship traveling in the opposite direction.

I wish we were as smart today as people were back in Jonah's time.

When they were going through great storms, the main thing they wanted to know was: which person is on this ship who doesn't need to be on board? Unlike so-called compassionate Christians who welcome rebellion by saying, "No problem, you can stay with us," the mariners tossed Jonah over the side of the boat. When Jonah was thrown overboard, a big fish swallowed him alive. Desperately alone in the gurgling belly of the fish, Jonah soon discovered that doing things his way was not working in his favor. He quickly realized that unless he repented and sought God's mercy, he would die in the belly of that fish. I can picture him shaking his head in wonder, asking himself, *What was I thinking? I just should have done what God asked me to do.* I'm sure he cried out to God something like, "Please get me out of here. I don't know why in the world I thought I could do this thing on my own. Forgive me."

God responded in mercy, and the fish vomited Jonah onto dry land. This time Jonah refused to waver, swiftly traveling and preaching whatever the Lord had originally told him to say. The king of Nineveh responded encouragingly to Jonah's message by instructing the entire city of Nineveh to fast, and as Jonah predicted, God spared the city. I'm sure Jonah had some time to think while he was alone in the belly of the fish. It was there, alone in the frightening darkness, that he discovered that God will have His way whether we follow or not.

God is sovereign, and He can and will do whatever He pleases. Therefore we must trust Him and lean not on our own understanding (Prov. 3:5). Don't fall prey to the desire to try to figure everything out. Repent for yielding to the temptation of doing things your own way. I believe the greatest definition of sin is found in Isaiah 53:6, which says, "All we like sheep have gone astray; we have turned, every one, to his own way."

Trust God, and He will deliver you. It brings me great peace to know that no matter where I am, whatever I may be facing, or whatever I am going through, I know God is going to deliver me. I can confidently declare, like the three Hebrew young men in the book of Daniel, that even if God doesn't deliver me, I still won't bow to the idols of this world (3:18). Yes, God will deliver you, but even if He doesn't, will you bow your knee to your own way? I, for one, will not!

There are many purported Christians who are just going through the motions of Christian calisthenics. Don't kid yourself—you are either depending on God for everything or you are depending on Him for nothing. There is no middle ground. You can't play games with God. He already knows whether or not you trust Him; your trust is proven through your actions. God will always show Himself to the person who finally surrenders and takes up his cross and follows after Him. As long as you continue to play the Christian game or straddle the fence, He will remain as distant as the moon. That is why James said, "Draw near to God and He will draw near to you" (James 4:8). Drawing near to God doesn't mean merely praying a prayer. What it actually means is leaving what you *were* in order to embrace who He *is*.

Some time ago, my wife and I noticed some flies buzzing around inside our house. They would not leave the room but insisted on just buzzing around, that is, until they finally ran out of gas. Some of us are like those flies buzzing around life, trying to make it on our own—doing it our own way. Those flies taught me a great deal. They are the kind of flies you need not bother to kill. One moment they're buzzing, but soon enough they will all be dead.

Perhaps you are at a point in your life where you feel as though you are buzzing aimlessly around life. If so, stop trying to make it on your own. Stop trying to figure everything out. Get desperate enough to trust God by breaking away from all the busyness of your life and getting alone with God. Spend time meditating on the passages that pertain to your present situation. Go over them repeatedly until you envision yourself doing them. Remember, "faith comes by hearing, and hearing by the word of God" (Rom. 10:17). In order to continue to build trust in God, you must immerse yourself in His Word.

You won't find the doorway out of worrying by running around, asking everybody and their brother about how to transform your life. You only find it when, like those dead flies, you spin yourself out in desperation and cry, "I'm done trying to do this on my own. I'm not running around anymore. I'm depending on God."

The benefits are well worth it because God has orchestrated a fabulous future for you. Your future with God may not be comfortable or trouble-free, but it will be fabulous because He is the architect, and the Chief Planner is with your every move.

—∞—

In the book of Nahum, alone with God, Nahum received God's revenge against His enemies; while in Habakkuk 1, alone with God, Habakkuk beheld the vicious Chaldean army; and in Zephaniah 1, alone with God, Zephaniah was commanded to "be silent."

chapter thirteen

EXCITING ESTABLISHMENT
OF WHO I AM

Whether in a peaceful corner of your apartment, settled beneath a grove of shady oak trees, or nestled within a bedroom closet, by spending time alone with God you will discover who you truly are. Alone with God and His Word was the only way Jesus discovered His identity. On a significant day in His life, Jesus entered the synagogue and stood up to read.

He was handed the book of the prophet Isaiah. And when He had opened the book, He found the place where it was written: "The Spirit of the LORD is upon Me, because He has anointed Me to preach the gospel to the poor; He has sent Me to heal the brokenhearted, to proclaim liberty to the captives and recovery of sight to the blind, to set at liberty those who are oppressed; to proclaim the acceptable year of the LORD." Then He closed the book, and gave it back to the attendant and sat down. And the eyes of all who were in the synagogue were fixed on Him. And He began to say to them, "Today this Scripture is fulfilled in your hearing." (Luke 4:17–21)

Jesus discovered the Scriptures' exciting establishment of His identity and He fulfilled it. Abraham discovered his identity at the ripe old age of ninety-nine when God appeared and revealed His plan for future generations (Gen. 17:1). Moses discovered his identity in one dramatic encounter when God told him, "I will send you to Pharaoh that you may bring My people, the children of Israel, out of Egypt" (Ex. 3:10). Jesus, Abraham, and Moses each discovered and embraced their new identities, and so can you. But where do we uncover our new identity?

FIND YOUR IDENTITY IN THE TRUTH OF SCRIPTURE

Your identity is hidden within the pages of God's Word. Listen to me carefully: *you will never find your identity in a crowd.* I don't think I can illustrate it any more emphatically than this. I lived my whole life afraid of me. I had no clue who I truly was, and I didn't know what I truly believed. I had no confidence about anything, and absolutely no encouragement about anything. I didn't know what was right; I didn't know what was wrong. I had to begin to shape a belief system to know *what* I believed and *why* I believed it. I knew it wouldn't come from my upbringing; I knew it wouldn't come from my mom, my dad, or even my grandparents. But after receiving Christ as my Lord and Savior I knew my new identity was found in one place—the Word of

God. The book of Hebrews tells us, "He takes away the first that He may establish the second" (10:9).

As Jesus, our prime example, set aside the first to establish the second, so I had to set aside who I was in order to embrace the exciting establishment of who I now was—a person who had been set free from God's wrath through Jesus' sacrifice. In Christ, I am a new creature; the old things have passed away, and all things have become new (2 Cor. 5:17).

SET ASIDE WHO YOU WERE SO YOU CAN BE WHO YOU ARE

You must set aside the person you used to be in order to establish your new identity in Christ. If you desire to embrace your new identity, then you must also be willing to relinquish the old one—the person you used to be. The Bible clearly tells us that our old self is dead and was crucified with Christ (Gal. 2:20). When you give up who you were, you then can walk in who you are in Christ. Understand this: you can never embrace your new life until you surrender the old. If all you want to do is to hang little ornaments on your life's rotting tree, you'll be like a struggling, frustrated Charlie Brown at Christmastime. But if you lay the ax at the root of the tree and establish who you are in Christ, you'll see the exciting establishment of a new life.

John the Baptist said it like this, "Produce fruit in keeping with repentance. . . . The axe is already at the root of the trees, and every tree that does not produce good fruit will be cut down and thrown into the fire" (Luke 3:8–9 NIV). Even if you're afraid of the unknown, you have to take a step toward change. If you don't face yourself today, you will do it someday in the near future.

I will be the first to admit that it can be a bit scary to completely abandon our past. It may not be easy to face ourselves because, for the most part, we are not ready to face what will be unearthed. As spiritual and emotional archeologists, we don't know what secrets we will stumble upon. We don't ask a lot of questions about our new life in Christ because we're afraid of the answers we might hear. But if we are going to surrender our lives to God, we must wholly embrace our new identity.

Jonathan Edwards, the leader of New England's Great Awakening, penned these words: "In close meditation, prayer and conversing with God, when alone and separated from the world, a true Christian doubtless delights . . . to converse with God in solitude and this also has peculiar advantages for fixing his heart, for fixing what is inside him."

You may argue, "But I'm too busy! On Monday I go shopping, on Tuesday I play golf, and on Wednesday afternoon I watch the grandkids." Do you realize the only thing you're doing is finding more and more excuses not to get alone with the one who is your source of strength? That is Satan's plan, to keep us so occupied, *even serving in the church*, that we never break away to spend quality time alone with God.

How often have you observed a person's unaltered life and discovered they're still messing around? They're not ready to change; they're still holding on to yesterday's issues.

Like gold hidden inside the ruins of some ancient civilization, our lives are hidden in identity with Jesus Christ. It is only in the Word of God that you will discover what is written about you—that your one and only purpose is to do the will of God. In the pages of the Book, you will discover what you must believe. Spending quality time studying God's Word will change your attitude, your beliefs, everything about you.

After having helped many people for much of my life, I can tell you this: until an individual becomes very serious about the outcome of his life, nothing will change. A boy will turn fifteen, sixteen, eighteen, twenty, twenty-two, twenty-five, twenty-eight, and then thirty. He will marry, and a few years later, his wife will ask me, "What can I do to motivate my husband?" It's very simple: until he realizes that God places people in His path to cause them to become great in God's eyes, there isn't anything you can do for him except make certain you don't take any steps backward in your own life.

It is impossible for you to compromise your way into the will of God. It is impossible to compromise your way into a good marriage. Nowhere in life can you back up into what's right. You can't keep doing wrong and have everything right happen. As a matter of fact, it is what you sow that you ultimately reap (Gal. 6:7). A day must come when you're no longer afraid of finding out who God has declared you to be from the foundations of the world. Ask the Lord to guide you and show you who you are. Open His Word and watch the exciting establishment of your new identity, of who you are, unfold. Get ready for a change!

—◊◊◊—

In Haggai 1, alone with God, Haggai, the prophet to Zerubbabel, was told by God that Israel must consider her ways; while in Zechariah 2, alone with God, Zechariah conversed with an angel. And in Malachi 1, alone with God, the Father asked Malachi, as well as the nation of Israel, "Where is My honor?"

chapter fourteen

NIPPING NEGATIVITY

I*'ll never get this right! It just can't be done!* Those are typical, time-honored words, aren't they? According to author Jack Canfield, research indicates that the average person talks to himself thousands of times each day.[1] The downside? Eighty percent of our self-talk derives from negative thoughts that adversely influence our behavior. Most often, however, we don't challenge those thoughts. And as I am often known to say, any thought left unchallenged becomes an established fact inside you.

How often do we waste moments alone, mentally reliving hurtful memories from our past? How often do we displease God because we allow ourselves to believe the negative thoughts that ruthlessly bombard our minds?

Whenever we allow negative thoughts to hover over our mind like a swarm of harassing bees, they become beliefs that ultimately become strongholds in our lives. Left unchecked, strongholds become so loud they alter the words you speak, the ideas you contemplate, and even the manner in which you treat family and friends. In the quiet moments of my young life, I would constantly remember the mean voices that had been spoken to me by unloving people. My thought life was full of negative voices, replaying over and over like a defective CD in my mind. Decades later I still vividly remember the pounding voices that incarcerated me in the mental institution and have intermittently tried to revisit me over the years. Each time they've attempted to speak, I have silenced them.

To ignore and nip these negative voices forever, I don't simply memorize Scripture, as many would encourage. In effect, like a prudent business owner, I *employ* the Scriptures. The Bible is not just a book that contains helpful sayings for us to memorize. It is the power of God, and when we put it into practice, everything about our lives falls into place. I regularly assess my life and the issues that I face, peering into God's Word for the answers to those challenges, utilizing those passages, confessing them until I accept them as true. When I envision myself performing them on the inside, it will become evident in my life.

But to experience the power of God available to us in His Word, negative thoughts must be silenced. According to the *Encarta* dictionary, the word *silence* means an "absence of acknowledgment of something." If we're going to silence something, we must learn to ignore it. How can we ignore the presence of a voice within?

SILENCE THE VOICES WHEN YOU ARE ALONE

First of all, I discovered that the time to conquer these strongholds is when we are alone, because this is the time when these negative thoughts attack us most. And because negative thoughts are so strong when we're alone, we often try to avoid solitude by filling our lives with endless activity. But negative thoughts will always remain when they are welcomed, even in a crowd. Although they flow at a low voltage, they are always around, perhaps just not center stage for the moment. Often, like dreaded enemies, these negative thoughts will meet you the moment you get alone. However, you must get alone if you are going to overcome them.

As I began to use solitude to solidify God's Word in my life, instead of looking to others for my identity, I looked intently into the "law of liberty" (James 1:25). Once I discovered the power of solitude, my life was never the same. Over the years, I've watched people and noticed how very few construct their lives in a meaningful way and the vast majority merely exist, allowing life to pass them by. I've learned that if we don't discover our personal identity, we will simply exist in life never accomplishing a thing for God.

CONFRONT YOUR PROBLEMS

The way to success in life is not by avoiding your problems; it is by coming face-to-face with them. You must choose a time to confront your thoughts. If you don't choose the time, life will choose it for you, particularly when you're in the middle of your weakest hour. I'm convinced that if you wait for hidden issues to force themselves upon you, they will sabotage you in an unsuspected ambush. By deliberately controlling the moment of attack, you secure a moment of time when you are strong.

Since coming to Christ, I have always forced myself to confront my problems. I don't wait for the Goliaths of life to run; I chase them down. I've overcome most of the issues in my life by attacking them directly. And I always to do it when I am alone with God. By taking His Word, I can sever the enemy's head with one blow. Let me ask you: is there any alternative to fighting? Some refute, "I don't want to deal with that issue right now." Rightly so, but if you don't deal with it now, then when? When you think that way, you're postponing a major crisis. The day will ultimately arrive when you're not strong enough to deal with your weaknesses. Believe me when I tell you, the enemy shows no mercy. He is like a roaring lion, fitted with blade-sharp teeth to sink into whomever he may devour.

Our problems do not simply disappear. You either look for them when you're strong or they'll look for you when you're not.

Have you ever noticed that your thoughts run rampant when you're exhausted? When you are weak, thoughts begin to gnaw on you. Unceasingly, negative thoughts nibble and nip away at your mind. Sometimes we wonder how great men and women fell into sin; one moment they were so strong, then the next, so weak. Most often people fall when they become weary. Remember that even Jesus rested when He was tired (Matt. 8:18, 24). And incidentally, don't most people tend to believe that if they're not currently experiencing any problems, they must be living in the will of God? Nothing could be further from the truth. When you move into an area where hell doesn't want you to go, you'll have to nip the negative voices that surface like a fierce school of sharks. If you're in the will of God, you'll experience tremendous resistance, and there will be tremendous opportunities for loss. But don't be discouraged; you have already overcome.

Take a look at Jesus. He was in the will of God, yet voices of confusion screamed at Him, even during the events surrounding the crucifixion. Chaos broke out around Him; one of His apostles betrayed Him, the apostle Peter denied knowing Him, He was falsely accused to the Roman governor Pontius Pilate, He was mocked and beaten, and crowds kept zealously shouting, "Crucify Him; crucify Him!"

All of us deal with voices every day—voices of truth and voices of deception. I'm sure Jesus didn't sweat great drops of blood because He was being attacked by blissful, positive thoughts. No, the enemy was attempting to move Him off course—to not follow through with God's assignment for His life. But Jesus wouldn't budge. He ardently declared, "Not My will, but Yours, be done" (Luke 22:42). When alone with God, Jesus made the commitment to press beyond the pressure to quit and give up. He made the decision to obey God.

How can we get started silencing negative voices without feeling overwhelmed? Well, we shouldn't make the great mistake of trying to fix everything immediately. If you try to transform all the areas of your life at once, you will be like the frustrated little Dutch boy trying to plug all the holes in the dike at once.

Why not simply take one area of your life and stay with it every day until your enemy is destroyed? Imitate David, who said, "I pursued my enemies and overtook them; I did not turn back till they were destroyed" (Ps. 18:37 NIV).

FACE YOUR ENEMY WHEN HE'S THE SMALLEST

We must face our problems when they are small; otherwise they will multiply and be too much for us to master. To understand this, picture your front lawn. If you don't go out there and get rid of the one tiny dandelion shoot today, you'll wake up facing *hundreds* of them when you open your front door tomorrow. When God reveals a small problem to you, immediately deal with it before you wake up to a plethora of problems in the morning. As Leonardo da Vinci fittingly observed, "It is easier to resist at the beginning than at the end."

My life isn't compiled of great miraculous stories but of small, daily victories won by confronting my enemies when they were the smallest. By taking one area of life and pursuing my enemy in that area until I defeated him, I didn't give up until the negative voice was destroyed, using Scripture to beat the pants off the devil. Don't think you have to memorize a lot of scriptures to fight him; I didn't. As I wrote earlier, I *used* scriptures to protect my mind and slay Goliath.

Finding a specific scripture that silences a negative voice is quite easy. One of the most effective ways to accomplish this is the usage of a Bible concordance. Just find the word *anger*, for example, and read all the verses listed under that topic. You can write down verses that help you the most and carry them with you to confess throughout your day. But let me make a note here: please make sure that you are not taking verses out of context. Don't stand on any promise that God never intended for you to stand upon.

When I'm alone, I take a specific set of scriptures and write them down, confessing them into my voice recorder. As I meditate and confess them throughout the day, the pressures of life seem to fade away. As I confess God's Word, His promises become bigger than my circumstances. When I feel pressure, I apply the Word to that pressure because I've already applied my life to the Word. You see, I am part of the body of Christ, and since "His name is called The Word of God" (Rev. 19:13), then what God's Word says I am, I *am*.

Start Applying Your Life to the Word

Stop attempting to apply the Word to your life, and begin to apply your life to the Word. This principle is true because, although the Word never changes, your life constantly does. When people consider applying the Word to their lives, it's as though their focus is on saving their lives. But Jesus said, "Whoever desires to save his life will lose it, but whoever loses his life for My sake and the gospel's will save it" (Mark 8:35). In order to find more of me, I have to lose more of my identity with this world.

When Linda and I were dating, I took her to see my grandmother to introduce them. Unfortunately, at that time, my grandmother was dying. That day, as she lay on the couch, she called me near to say, "Robbie, you need to marry her."

I answered, "Well, Grandma, we're thinking about it."

She said, "No, you *need* to marry her."

I said, "Okay, Grandma."

She then confessed, "Robbie, I have something else I want to tell you. I just wanted you to know that you were always my favorite."

I started to cry.

She asked, "Why are you crying?"

I answered, "Because I always thought you hated me."

Out of thirty-two grandchildren, I was her favorite, but I didn't know it until she was dying. My grandma always loved me, but by the time I found out, it was way too late. There was nothing I could do because she died. And that's what happens with people. By the time they discover the truth about their relationship with God, they have missed out on so many blessings.

Rise up and be who you really are by nipping and forever silencing negative voices with the Word of God.

—∞—

As recorded in all four Gospels (Matthew, Mark, Luke, and John), alone with God, Jesus sought His Father's will, which eventually led Him to the cross and victory at the resurrection. In Acts 2, one hundred and twenty Christians witnessed the prophesied outpouring of the Holy Spirit. And in Romans, alone with God, Paul wrote to believers of potent Christian doctrine.

chapter fifteen

CONTROLLED COMBAT

The television newscaster's drone, irritable kids' complaints, dissatisfied neighbors, quarreling relatives, jealous coworkers, sensual music—there are endless varieties of voices daily contending for our hearts, souls, and minds. At this moment, what negative voices are speaking personally to *you?* And more importantly, what are you doing to combat them? In order to ignore these voices, you must enter into controlled combat against them.

In this chapter, we'll look at ten negative voices that try to derail you from obeying God. Although you may not be hearing all ten of these voices at the moment, I guarantee you will hear them at some point in time, so preparation is vital. Let's take an in-depth look at each one.

VOICE #1: THE VOICE OF FEAR

In heart-throbbing fright, Joshua's ten spies spread discouraging reports among the Israelite people, influencing them to fearfully withdraw from entering the Promised Land. Because the spies didn't silence the voice of fear, the Israelites wandered in the wilderness for forty monotonous years (Num. 13–14).

Today, if you don't obey God's Word, what do you have to look forward to? There is no alternative. Never stop obeying! Never stop pressing for more of God! Never stop venturing out there and writing your life story.

Faith is energized by dreaming about the future while fear gains its strength from rehearsing the past. Are you afraid you'll fail? If so, then fear has become your master. The minute the enemy offers an alternative option into the ring is the minute most people will fail. If you don't want to fail, never allow fear to address you. Always speak back. Notify fear exactly of what it is that you are going to do, and never, ever concede.

Confess this according to the Word of God: "I will succeed. Everything I put my hands to will prosper. Greater is He who is in me than he who is in the world. My delight and desire is in the Word of God. I will habitually meditate, ponder, and orally recite it both day and night, then I shall be like a tree that's planted by the rivers of water which sends out its shoots by the streams, whose leaves also shall not wither and whatever I put my hand to will prosper" (Deut. 28:8; 1 John 4:4; Ps. 1:2–3).

Don't think you can consistently tolerate fear, or that somehow when you wake up it will have mysteriously vanished. The way to deal with the voice of fear is to confront it head-on. But in order to confront it, you must target it as enemy prey. Yes, you must hunt it down! You must do everything you possibly can in order to find your fear, deal with it, and knock it out of your life.

How is this done? The key is to take the Scriptures and combat the harassing thoughts of fear, anxiety, and worry. Like a soldier preparing for war, you must put on the armor of God and fight. Although the battle is the Lord's, we must take the stones of God's Word and hurl them with the sling of God's grace to strike down our Goliath of fear.

What does it mean to put on the armor of God? When the Scriptures say to put on our spiritual armor, it implies a readiness for battle. We must decide to fight if we desire to win. You can't win a battle that you don't fight. One part of the armor is truth. Another is the sword of the Spirit, which is the Word of God, enabling us to rebuke the devil with His Word. Ephesians 6:11–17 describes our armor and commands us to put it on to face our daily battles with the enemy.

Read how one person fights the voice of fear:

God has proven His faithfulness to me over the years when I was in the midst of what I have to say has been the biggest struggle in my life—fear. You know, the fear that deceives you into believing that you can handle life's problems better than God. Fear that needs to be silenced as soon as you recognize it, with God's weapons, or it will tempt you into believing that God's arm is too short to rescue you . . . your family . . . your future.

Fear is a liar that tells you "God may be big enough to have a good plan for your future, but He certainly isn't big enough to perform it," which leads you to think, *I better rescue myself from this weak, scary place*. But I discovered that my feelings of strength and safety are fleeting. The truth is, I'm weak, and that's okay because Psalm 72:12 says that if we choose to call out to Him instead of ourselves in our neediness, He will help us: "For He delivers the needy when he calls out" [AMP]. I have to daily ask the Holy Spirit to remind me to accept my smallness and receive His bigness. That way, I silence the voice of fear, disabling it from its ability to paralyze me. Instead of feeling burdened, I'm free to praise Him joyfully and pray in all circumstances.

After spending time alone with the Lord, this is how one mother began to courageously ignore the voice of fear:

As our oldest son grew and entered the military, we had hoped this would help him find his way back to Christ. He loved God as a young boy, and then as he grew older, he began slipping away from God. He married a beautiful young woman who was from a family that didn't worship Christ. In fact, this cult totally denied the deity of Him.

As a mom, and feeling overwhelmed, I knew that I wasn't in faith for his return to Christ. My trust was in my circumstances and not His promise! One morning after praying, I was reminded that Christ had already done everything on the cross for me and my family and had given me *all power and authority* over this situation. I remember turning around in my family room and getting spitting mad at the devil and reminding him of God's promises for me and our son. Every day after that, I thanked God for my son and daughter-in-law knowing Him and their desire to love truth. It wasn't long until both of them gave their lives over to Christ and today are actively pursuing Him, plugged into a wonderful church and serving Him!

Now, that is something only a few people ever do. You won't find a lot of people who actually confront their fears. People think fear is too great to overcome and conclude they should suppress it rather than face it head-on. But if you don't deal with fear now, it will haunt you when God decrees that it's time to do something for His kingdom. At that moment, fear will say, "Nope, not this time. Don't trust God. He won't come through."

Most people will go up and down, back and forth, but they won't face off with the fear issue.

Silence the voice of fear.

Voice #2: The Voice of Yesterday

You are either a prisoner of your past or a pioneer of your future. How long are you going to allow your past to prevent you from doing what God has called you to do? One of the things I have discovered in my life's journey is that there is no future in a person's past. There is nothing there; there is nothing for you to embrace, hold on to, or celebrate. You can't do anything about what's behind, so let it go. God does not give me the right to allow my past to keep me from pioneering the future that He desires for my family and me.

Here is how one woman ignored an influential voice from her family's past in order to secure a promising future for her children:

I believe my success in raising my three daughters was totally based on my trust in God. Their father said that they would not be able to go to college because of our divorce. I got on my knees and called out to God, saying, "Lord God, it's not what their earthly father says but it's what You have to say. I ask You in the name of Jesus to make a way for all three of my daughters to go to college. In fact, I give them to you!"

One week later, a patient at St. James Hospital prophesied that my children, who were all in elementary school at the time, would go to college and do well. She saw my middle daughter as an attorney, which she now is in Los Angeles. My youngest daughter will graduate from Northwestern Medical School next spring, and my eldest will complete her PhD this fall. They are all saved and attend church in their areas. I thank God for answered prayer.

Instead of listening to the voice of yesterday, spend time alone to meditate and confess scriptures such as "Choose life, that both you and your descendants may live" (Deut. 30:19) and "I focus on this one thing: Forgetting the past and looking forward to what lies ahead, I press on to reach the end of the race and receive the heavenly prize for which God, through Christ Jesus, is calling us" (Phil. 3:13–14 NLT).

Silence the voice of yesterday.

VOICE #3: THE VOICE OF DOUBT

Regardless of what you are going through, remember God's Word is always true. The Bible tells us, "God is not a man, that he should lie, nor a son of man, that he should change his mind. Does he speak and then not act? Does he promise and not fulfill?" (Num. 23:19 NIV). And to Thomas, Jesus instructed, "Stop doubting and believe" (John 20:27 NIV).

Doubt is the tool used by evil to destroy God's timing in your life. It is a rare individual who has never needed specific direction or a certain amount of finances by a prescribed deadline. Read what happened to one woman who decided to spend time with God and trust His direction:

I decided to go on a mission trip to Haiti in December 2006. I did not have the extra finances to pay for the trip, and I had just asked people to sponsor my trip to Kenya in September, only a few months earlier. I thought that if I worked an extra job on the weekends, I could save enough money to pay for the trip.

After spending time reading the Word of God and attending church, I felt that I should let my boss know that I was working another job to raise money for the trip. I did not want him to find out from someone else or think that I was leaving my permanent job.

When I told my boss what I was doing and why, he said he did not want me working another job. He asked what the trip would cost, and I told him it was $1,295. He responded, "That's all? We'll take care of that for you. I don't want you working another job and burning the candle at both ends."

I was speechless! So much pressure was instantly relieved when I told my boss about my situation. Spending time with God not only led to finances for the mission trip but also led me to a deeper trust in God's ability to provide for me without trying to work it out myself.

If this woman had doubted God's direction, she would have foregone His surprising provision for a trip through which she could benefit others for eternity. Since it's impossible for God to lie, do you realize that the Word of God will remain true no matter what you are facing?

Don't let the actions of others cause you to doubt God's integrity. I learned this some time ago when the orderly who led me to the Lord backslid two months after I came to Christ. Now, that wasn't a good day in my life. After that, the other man who taught me more about God's Word than anyone else also backslid, right before my eyes. And so we must make the decision that we're going to trust the Word of God no matter what happens to any human being. Jesus taught us, "If you hold to my teaching, you are really my disciples. Then you will know the truth, and the truth will set you free" (John 8:31–32 NIV). No matter what you are facing, you must refuse to doubt God's Word. If He said it, then He will do it. Here's another testimony:

About eighteen years ago, I was diagnosed with an extreme case of TMJ. The MRI showed that the discs in the joints of my jaws were disintegrating. The doctors told me that if I did not have the surgery to replace my discs with plastic discs, by the time I was forty, I would have no mobility in my jaws. However, if I had the surgery, the doctors promised me a life on painkillers.

I decided not to have the surgery, and I chose to speak the Word, as I have been taught according to Mark 23. During that time, my jaws would lock shut and the pain was continuous and severe.

There were times when people would come to church with healing ministries. I would cry, thinking I had no faith for a miracle cure for my jaws. I didn't receive a miracle, or so I thought.

For years I spoke the Word, day after day, hour after hour. During that time, I was in desperate need of braces. The crookedness of my teeth was compounding the TMJ issue. But orthodontists told me my jaws were too weak to sustain braces.

I kept speaking the Word.

Here I am, eighteen years later (over forty years old), and I am pain-free. I have straight teeth and full mobility of my jaws. I did receive a miracle. It may not have occurred during a church service, but as I spoke the Word, God watched over His Word to perform it.

I am healed. I did not give up, even though it took years for my miracle to manifest. I am thankful I was able to transform my life along with my physical body by confessing the Word of God.

The Word of God remains true regardless of what you or anyone else is going through.

Silence the voice of doubt.

Voice #4: The Voice of Pride

Greatness becomes yours the moment you become small in your own eyes.

It is too bad Israel's King Saul couldn't understand this important truth. Before becoming the king of Israel, Saul was a humble man; afterward, he began to believe his own press release, which ultimately ruined his life. Through the prophet Samuel, God told Saul, "When you were little in your own eyes, were you not head of the tribes of Israel? And did not the LORD anoint you king over Israel?" (1 Sam. 15:17). When we are small in our own eyes, God can use us to do great things, but the moment we become big in our own eyes, God resists us (1 Pet. 5:5).

James 4:10 says, "Humble yourselves in the sight of the Lord, and He will lift you up." I completely enjoy the refreshing realization that I don't need to try to create anything out of my life; if God doesn't do it, then I don't want it to be done. If it doesn't happen, I don't need it and I don't want it.

Give up your opinion of yourself; God's opinion is the only one that matters. God resists the proud.

Silence the voice of pride.

VOICE #5: THE VOICE OF SELF

The greatest giant you'll ever face is you. "I never met a man who gave me as much trouble as myself," admitted evangelist Dwight L. Moody.

I couldn't agree more with what Mr. Moody wisely perceived. I've never met any demon as strong as my flesh. It was Charles Spurgeon who quipped, "If the fur is being rubbed the wrong way, then turn the cat around." If I'm hearing a voice of resistance to God's Word, I need to identify the reason and deal with it. God is never the one who needs to change. No, it's always me.

Galatians 5:17 proclaims, "The flesh lusts against the Spirit, and the Spirit against the flesh; and these are contrary to one another, so that you do not do the things that you wish." Have you discovered yet that your flesh craves the opposite of what your spirit craves? There is always a brutal battle between your flesh and your spirit. This is a battle that will continue until you see Jesus.

Crucifying the flesh does not mean taking out a whip and striking your back thirty-nine times. Crucifying your flesh means harnessing negative thoughts and bringing them into subjection to God's Word (2 Cor. 10:4–5). For instance, when a Bible verse exposes a wrong thought, instead of embracing the wrong thought, embrace God's Word. This way, you crucify the thought that displeases God.

The Bible says to "clothe yourself with the Lord Jesus Christ (the Messiah), and make no provision for [indulging] the flesh [put a stop to thinking about the evil cravings of your physical nature] to [gratify its] desires (lusts)" (Rom. 13:14 AMP). In other words, starve your flesh. For example, if you decide to leave sexual immorality behind, you must rid yourself of anything that gives you an opportunity to fulfill the desires of your flesh: the movies you watch, the people you associate with, the magazines you purchase, or whatever it may be. Sever it completely from your life, then break away and get alone with God.

Jesus said, "The Spirit gives life; the flesh counts for nothing. The words I have spoken to you are spirit and they are life" (John 6:63 NIV). Deal with your weaknesses today—in your marriage, in your parenting, and in yourself—so that they won't intensify into bigger giants tomorrow.

Silence the voice of self.

VOICE #6: THE VOICE OF OFFENSE

If you refuse to forgive others, you burn the bridge you must cross the moment you need forgiveness.

Offense does not mean that you're mad; offense means that you've chosen to respond to life contrary to what is written. When you're offended by something in God's Word, you're saying, "You know what? I don't agree with that." That's why Jesus often asked people, "Does this offend you?" John 6:61 says, "When Jesus knew in Himself that His disciples complained about this, He said to them, 'Does this offend you?'"

When you disagree with a Bible teacher, you can follow the example of your Christian brothers and sisters before you who "received the word with all readiness, and searched the Scriptures daily to find out whether these things were so" (Acts 17:11). Go to the Scriptures. The Scriptures mean what they say, and they do not contradict one another. Search them out. It's as simple as that.

Become interested in the whole counsel of God, studying the Scriptures to see whether these things are so. One reason God gave us the Bible is to help us.

Silence the destructive voice of offense.

Voice #7: The Voice of Greed

Unless we embrace God's purpose for prosperity, greed will always be our looming master. Every good and perfect gift comes from the Lord, even our finances. If God has blessed you with wealth to any degree, He requires that you sow into the lives of others. He does this to silence the voice of greed. Jesus said it like this, "No one can serve two masters. . . . You cannot serve both God and Money" (Matt. 6:24 NIV).

The only two chapters in all of the Scriptures that are dedicated solely to the financial arena are 2 Corinthians 8 and 9. In these two chapters, the apostle Paul reminds us that whatever you give will return to you, but with this emphatic admonition: "Remember this: Whoever sows sparingly will also reap sparingly, and whoever sows generously will also reap generously" (2 Cor. 9:6 NIV).

Proverbs 11:24 says, "There is one who scatters, yet increases more; and there is one who withholds more than is right, but it leads to poverty." You must learn to continue to sow generously, or else by your withholding, you'll be led to poverty rather than to prosperity.

Jesus commands us, "Go into all the world and preach the good news to all creation" (Mark 16:15 NIV). This highlights the purpose of finances for advancing the kingdom of God. How can anyone go unless their financial needs are met? It takes tremendous finances to travel the world. Keep giving and embrace God's purpose for prosperity.

Silence the voice of greed.

VOICE #8: THE VOICE OF BETRAYAL

The voice of betrayal will tempt you to harm someone by revealing something about him or her to another. The voice of betrayal will whisper *break your promise*. The voice of betrayal will bring you to a place of deceiving others. The voice of betrayal will tell you to be disloyal.

Loyalty is never as beautiful as the day betrayal rears its ugly head. Loyalty is like insurance: it has no value until the day betrayal appears, and then loyalty is proven.

A number of years ago, some water flooded our basement. Although it was fresh water, it was flawed because it was someplace it wasn't supposed to be. Without asking a single question or arguing with us about it, our insurance company gave us a check to cover the damage.

When someone tells me, "I'm a loyal person," my response is, "We'll see." A loyal person remains true even after he's finished getting what he wanted from you. Matthew 26–27 portrays the story of

Judas Iscariot, a disloyal man who decided to betray Jesus. As Judas approached Jesus, Jesus asked, "Friend, why have you come?" (Matt. 26:50). Afterward, the authorities Judas had led to Jesus immediately seized Him. Remorseful that he had betrayed his innocent friend, Judas left and hanged himself.

Betrayal will stop you in your tracks. If you have betrayed someone, please repent. Get alone with God and repent right now. Ask Him to forgive you, and if possible, ask the other person to forgive you. Choose today to never betray another person in your life again. Determine to be known as Jesus was known—a person of "integrity [who isn't] swayed by men" (Matt. 22:16 NIV).

Silence the voice of betrayal.

VOICE #9: THE VOICE OF DENIAL

Personal honesty is the beginning of permanent change. Even though the apostle Paul taught the grace of God and the forgiveness of our sins, and additionally instructed how we are the righteousness of God in Christ Jesus, he was the one who also said, "Christ Jesus came into the world to save sinners, of whom I am chief" (1 Tim. 1:15). Paul didn't deny that he was a sinner; in fact, he even called himself the worst of all sinners.

People love to live in denial, don't they? Many individuals prefer to describe themselves after the moment God saved them by grace instead of depicting themselves from the moment they needed grace.

You may say, "But according to 2 Corinthians 5:21, I'm not a sinner. I'm the righteousness of God." That's true, but don't ever forget that you enjoy righteousness on loan in Christ. In and of yourself, you are not righteous; you have been justified by the blood of Christ. You are legally declared righteous before God, but in and of yourself, before regeneration, you were an enemy and hater of God. All you need to do is look around to realize that Christians haven't been perfected yet. What we have is the down payment of that righteousness. Consequently, we *are* the righteousness of God in Christ Jesus, but we still must resist the devil daily.

Let's never live in denial like the man I once met who was always drunk but consistently resisted help. Disavowing any guilt, he would claim, "Well, I'm the righteousness of God." That was the same as saying, "Man, I don't have any faults. I don't know what you're talking about." I'm sad to report—no one could help him!

Internal honesty is the beginning of external change. When I'm honest with God, I become honest with myself, and then I'm able to be honest with others. When we're honest with ourselves, we won't react arrogantly when people correct us, knowing there's probably some truth to what they say. How often have you encountered people who want to talk behind someone else's back? Do you know what's wrong with that, among other things? The moment someone opens his mouth to condemn another person, he reveals something negative about himself. Through slandering someone else, he opens up his life to eventual scrutiny. Doesn't he realize he needs forgiveness too?

The reason I can forgive you is because I also need forgiveness. Now, that doesn't mean I'll forget what you've done, because there are always relational consequences for all behavior. Consequences don't just go away because you want them to.

The apostle Paul explained it like this: "Do you not know that those who run in a race all run, but one receives the prize? Run in such a way that you may obtain it. And everyone who competes for the prize is temperate in all things. Now they do it to obtain a perishable crown, but we for an imperishable crown. Therefore I run thus: not with uncertainty. Thus I fight: not as one who beats the air. But I discipline my body and bring it into subjection, lest, when I have preached to others, I myself should become disqualified" (1 Cor. 9:24–27).

Silence the voice of denial.

VOICE #10: THE VOICE OF DECEPTION

If truth does not conquer deception in your life, evil will continually triumph.

Isn't it true that we're almost always the last ones to catch sight of what's really going on in our own lives? I wish it wasn't that way, but it's true. In most cases, people will become angry the moment you begin to tell them the truth about themselves. When the apostle Paul encountered this, he asked, "Have I now become your enemy by telling you the truth?" (Gal. 4:16 NIV). He was trying to say, "I'm not your enemy because I told you the truth. I just might be the only friend you've ever had."

At one point, the apostle Paul had to face off with the apostle Peter for being a hypocrite. He said, "I opposed [Peter] to his face, because he was clearly in the wrong" (Gal. 2:11 NIV). Can you imagine? And we won't even confront people who have committed obvious wrong, but the apostle Paul faced off with an individual who committed a *subtle* wrong. And he didn't stop there—he rebuked Peter publicly and then wrote about it in a book!

James urges us, "Do not merely listen to the word, and so deceive yourselves. Do what it says. . . . If anyone considers himself religious and yet does not keep a tight rein on his tongue, he deceives himself and his religion is worthless" (James 1:22, 26 NIV). The apostle John puts it very candidly: "If we claim to be without sin, we deceive ourselves and the truth is not in us" (1 John 1:8 NIV).

The truth is important. Silence the voice of deception at all costs.

Certainly, not all of these voices are speaking to you right now, but when you get alone, pinpoint the ones that are. Once you've identified them, attack them in controlled combat with God's Word until you have stopped them from neutralizing your effectiveness.

Challenge and silence negative voices on the battlefield immediately.

—m—

In 1 Corinthians 1, alone with God, Paul wrote that there should be no divisions in the church. In the entire book of 2 Corinthians, alone with God, the same apostle addressed several of the churches' problems and trials. And in Galatians 5, alone with God, once again Paul wrote to remind us of our freedom in Christ.

chapter sixteen

SOLITUDE OR SECLUSION?

I'll handle this on my own, the young mother thought following a confusing night with relatives, a night of undeserved insults, subtle criticism, and nagging offense. But when we, like this young mother, no longer seek counsel from others, the devil begins to pummel us. Have you ever known someone who listened to others for a while but then decided to withdraw from relationships, saying, "Well, I'm going to deal with these things by myself?" Instead of advancing toward a positive direction, you begin to see her life spin out of control.

GOD PREPARES YOU WHEN YOU ARE ALONE

When the enemy wants to destroy you, he forces you to seclusion, but when God wants to prepare you, He calls you to be alone.

When God wants to prepare you, He calls you aside. Softly He whispers, *come over here. I want to form you.* When the enemy wants to destroy you, he forces you away from everyone. You become a person who rarely spends time with anyone anymore. You become a person who doesn't want company because it seems as though every person you're around becomes a greater hassle than they've ever been before.

What is the difference between solitude and seclusion? Are they the same thing, or are they completely different? I've been through them both. One was a friend that I thought was an enemy; the other was an enemy that I was sure was a friend. Seclusion causes us to walk in deception, while solitude exposes the truth of who we are. Solitude forces a person to face reality. Seclusion allows a person to run from the issues of life.

It's important for us to know that some of the things we think are very good are really not good at all. Likewise, some things that test us may just be the very things that are necessary for you and me to grow in the Lord. From a distant perspective, solitude and seclusion appear to be twins. But with closer examination, they have nothing whatsoever in common. You see, seclusion can be very *de*structive, while solitude is *con*structive.

GOD WANTS US TO BE ALONE, BUT NOT LONELY

Seclusion ultimately leads to loneliness. Loneliness is a powerful feeling of emptiness and disconnectedness. In other words, loneliness is a negative state where a person feels unfulfilled. Perhaps the bitterest form of loneliness is when someone is surrounded by people yet feels completely alone.

Loneliness is being disconnected or alienated from others so that it feels difficult or even impossible to have any form of meaningful human contact. But at its heart, loneliness is something other than simply desiring more friends. Loneliness is not the absence of people; loneliness is the absence of taking the time to be with God. The Bible tells us, "In Your presence is fullness of joy" (Ps. 16:11).

Solitude, on the other hand, is the state of being alone without experiencing a sense of loneliness. Solitude is a positive and constructive state of aloneness with God. Therefore, solitude gives us a chance to regain His perspective instead of living from our own subjective perspective. Being alone with God renews us for the challenges of life. It allows us to return to a position of allowing God to guide us, rather than schedules and demands from without, which often feverishly drive our lives.

As one individual attests:

Spending times alone with God are my most crucial and important times during the day. When I get away to really focus on God and spend time reading His Word, praying, and singing to God, it is my fuel for the day. . . . It is during those alone-times when my faith is strengthened, God's Word speaks to my heart, my focus is re-entered, I am refreshed and strengthened, and I get a lot of ideas and ways to be productive.

If you and I will ever achieve any level of fulfillment, we must develop the discipline of solitude. Solitude actually opens the door of possibility; it allows us to think outside the box in which others have enclosed us. Fulfillment is a direct result of solitude. For years, I thought solitude was my enemy. I mused, *why in the world do I have to spend this time alone? This drives me up a wall.* But later I found solitude to be my greatest ally. It was alone that I drew close to God, and it was alone that I conquered most of the fears that plagued my life.

Conversely, I initially believed that seclusion was my friend. Ultimately, I discovered it wasn't my friend at all, but one of my greatest enemies. I didn't understand that seclusion was continually stealing from me, while solitude was giving me a constructive, productive life.

Time and again I must be on guard since it's easy to go to opposite extremes by being alone too much and secluding myself. Not being a very external person, I don't feel a great need to see or talk to most people. What I really desire is to be left alone. But giving into that desire would only lead me into increased seclusion. At times I must intentionally force myself out of the house. Sometimes I stop to check whether it is God who is pulling me aside to be alone with Him or if it is the devil who is forcing me into seclusion. At those times I ask myself, *for what purpose do I desire to be alone?* When I cannot find the answer, I realize that I'm approaching a state of seclusion where my faith can and will be attacked.

Never allow yourself to be forced into a state of seclusion. If you do, you'll start thinking strange thoughts. Thinking strange thoughts isn't so bad until you start thinking that you're right and the whole world is against you. That's what happened to Elijah. Looking around at all the wicked, idolatrous people, he started thinking, *I am the only one left who is faithful to God.* I can just hear God laughing at the prophet's absurd observation. God responded to Elijah by saying, in essence, "Sorry, pal. If you would have gotten out of the house a little bit, maybe you would have figured out that there were seven thousand others who had never bowed their knee to Baal either" (1 Kings 19:14–18).

You not only need to break away from the busyness of life, but you also need to break away from the world and get around other believers. If you seclude yourself, all you need to do is write down how many years you have left in days, then take your pencil and put a minus sign behind it. Next, start subtracting the number of days you have secluded yourself, because in so doing, you shortened your life. It's so important, even as early as your teens, to start building your life with people; otherwise, when you're old, you'll be the lonely one who shuffles toward the window to watch the cars pass by because no one is coming to visit you.

It is so important to build your life with people. Don't ever think you're doing what is right by living apart from others. There is a benefit in being alone with God when He draws you apart to shed you of that which is wrong and inject you with what is right. But other than that, you must be interdependently minded rather than independently minded. The Bible tells us that we are the body of Christ, and being a part of the body requires us to function well with the other members of the body (1 Cor. 12:12). If we seclude ourselves, we are not fulfilling our unique role.

One person benefits from her relationships in this way:

A lot of fears and negatives come pretty naturally when I'm alone, but I like finding out those things so I can identify what I'm dealing with. I usually start praying and writing about them, then I start looking up scriptures and write some more. Clarity definitely comes when I'm alone, but sometimes so does confusion. In these moments when I'm unable to figure things out, I feel like I need to ask somebody to help me see the answer so I won't stay the same.

Some of the people I choose to be around are men who mentor me. I remember once pleading with them, "Oh, please, help me! I just can't believe how much I'm being persecuted." And do you know what they told me, these men I look to for solace and comfort, these men who have come alongside me to strengthen me? Laughing, they said, "We don't want to hear about any of this. We just need to know one thing."

"What's that?" I asked.

"When you're persecuted, do they spell your name right in the paper?"

"Yes."

"Good. You never want people to think someone else is being persecuted."

We must go through those days, because those days will make us stronger. Those days will either develop you or they will destroy you—but it's your choice. Will you get better or will you get bitter? Will they destroy you or will they make you a champion?

God will call you aside to test you. Did you know that God actually called Jesus aside to come face-to-face with the devil? The Bible tells us, "Jesus was led by the Spirit into the desert to be tempted by the devil. After fasting forty days and forty nights, he was hungry. The tempter came to him and said, 'If you are the Son of God, tell these stones to become bread.' Jesus answered, 'It is written: "Man does not live on bread alone, but on every word that comes from the mouth of God."' . . . Then the devil left him, and angels came and attended him" (Matt. 4:1–4, 11 NIV).

Temptation is for our destruction while testing is for our promotion. Testing helps you grow to the place where no matter what happens, you are not moved—you must stand firm. Don't believe that if you avoid temptation your character is strong. Just because you avoided temptation this time doesn't mean there won't be a day when you come face-to-face with it again, because you will.

YOUR LIFE WILL BE DEFINED BY YOUR RESPONSE TO TEMPTATION

James 1:12 says a person is blessed who endures temptation "for when he has been approved, he will receive the crown of life which the Lord has promised to those who love Him." When you're tempted, show the integrity and dignity that made you keep your word even though it hurt: a righteous man "swears to his own hurt and does not change" (Ps. 15:4).

During the early years of my walk with God, I didn't fully understand what was happening—even though I thought I was experiencing loneliness, somehow I knew I wasn't. So I stayed beneath the solitude, refusing to allow it to become full-blown loneliness. You must stay under the solitude while the Holy Spirit works inside your life because the day will come when you will bypass that season of your life. Then, like a beautiful monarch butterfly, you will finally emerge. The only question is, did you learn what God was attempting to teach you? If not, get ready, because you are going to repeat the test.

Sometimes you might not recognize that God is working in your life through a test, so you might start doing everything you can to reach out to heaven for help. You might think that hell is trying to beat you bloody, but in reality, heaven has its hand on you; God is leading you through the valley of the shadow of death. Remember this: when God wants to prepare you, He calls you to be alone. When He wants to promote you, He tests you.

For example, Lot's destruction was scheduled the moment he isolated himself. In Genesis 13, Lot and Abram encountered a problem. Lot was a man who was blessed because of his association with his uncle Abram. He had been moving around with Abram and his family, and because the land wasn't big enough for both of their herds, these herdsmen began to quarrel. Wanting to quell the dissention, Abram said to Lot, "Let's not have any quarreling between you and me, or between your herdsmen and mine" (v. 8 NIV). He then allowed his nephew to take first choice of the land.

Why in the world did Lot think he deserved to take what he wanted when his relationship with Abram was the very thing that caused him to be blessed in the first place? But that's what he did. While Abram lived in the land of Canaan, Lot chose to pitch his tent toward Sodom. While Abram pursued God, Lot lusted after Sodom, a city filled with corruption and depravity. You see, Lot decided to live life the way he wanted to, secluding himself from other believers. When Lot decided to go on his own, he didn't move toward better things; he moved toward destruction.

Mark my words: if you study the lives of people who have secluded themselves, you will discover they move further away from God. Their relationship with God did not grow. In fact, it became almost nonexistent. It happened all the way back in history to the book of Genesis, and it's been continuing ever since. I am absolutely bewildered at finding that some people will move toward a certain believer to gain God's blessing, but when they receive it, they move away and pitch their tent elsewhere. When I see this happen to others, I find that *where* they pitch their tent plainly reveals their motives all the way back to the beginning.

These experiences are painful when you have given of yourself into another person's life. For years, you may have taught someone the things of God only to discover he wasn't in it for God. For years, you have upheld him and under girded him in prayer. Then when he experienced a little bit of success, he pitched his tent in the exact opposite direction than you or God were heading.

GOD CALLS US TO INTERDEPENDENCE

God has not called us to independence, but He has called us to interdependence. Please realize that hell desires for you to become independent in your thinking: to believe that you can get somewhere and achieve something on your own. That is why I laugh when someone actually says, "I'm a self-made millionaire." It is just not true. Those who believe they can get to where God wants them to go on their own are only fooling themselves. People have the idea that being independent is a good thing. Sure, it may be great to have an independent country, but you are part of a community as well as a body and therefore must link arms, not only with your authorities, but also with your brothers and sisters in Christ to the glory of God.

First Corinthians 12 explains that you and I are only part of many parts of the body. By myself, I'm not the total of anything. As long as I continue to move in conjunction with the body of Christ, I'm able to receive all God has for me. The moment I begin to move away from the body, I become like a little finger trying to write all by itself. Just as one finger needs the other four on a hand to hold a pen and write, you and I need one another to walk through life the way God intended for us to walk.

An individual who secludes himself lives independently, not interdependently. Which way do you live? Do you tend to seclude yourself?

If so, take seriously the truths I am sharing with you. Seclusion is a device of the devil. He recognizes that his only way of defeating you is to seclude you from others. Make a decision to reconnect and link arms with other lovers of God. When you do, your life will never be the same.

Additionally, there is a more subtle form of seclusion than disconnection from people. It is known as emotional isolation. People can experience emotional isolation even if they have a well-functioning social network. Population-based research indicates that one in five middle-aged and elderly men, ages fifty to eighty, are emotionally isolated, which means they're defined as having no one in which to confide. Of those who do have someone to confide in, eight out of ten confide only in their spouses. Men who have no one to confide in are less likely to feel alert and strong. If they have no one to confide in, men are less likely to feel calm, energetic, or happy. They regularly feel contrary and are more likely to be depressed, sad, tired, and worn out.

May I speak to all the wives who are reading this for a moment? Instead of always pleading with your husband, "I just want you to be alone with you," why not instead encourage your husband to build positive relationships with other men? Some wives border on control when they want all of their husband's attention. What women do not realize is that they are mothering and actually smothering their husbands. "Oh, he's just kind of a homebody." No, he's not. He's isolated. And you may be the cause.

Choose Solitude Instead of Seclusion

Remember this: our motive for being alone will determine whether heaven or hell meets us there. Why do you want to be alone? Proverbs tells us, "A man who isolates himself seeks his own desire; he rages against all wise judgment" (18:1). When I isolate myself, I'm seeking my own desires; I'm doing my own thing; I'm no longer interested in wise counsel. I am working against what God wants me to confront. I'm pulling away because I don't want to face prospective pain. I'm doing everything I can to avoid further rejection.

When I seclude myself, negative thinking continues working on me until I am offended with God, which is often revealed by being offended with the authority God has placed over my life. No longer do I embrace the Word of God. I'll even tell people, "Oh, I love the Word. I just can't handle people." Or, I'll even say, "I love the Word of God, but I tell you, it's just *those* people. . . ." Offense is nothing more than refusing to embrace God's response to a particular situation or person. By secluding yourself, you are now seeking your own desires, and no longer God's; the Bible says clearly that you are raging against the counsel of God. Be sure to regularly choose solitude instead of seclusion, seeking God as David did, to "be still, and know that I am God" (Ps. 46:10). Friends, it is vital that you spend moments alone with God because unless you do, seclusion will control your life as it has for so many.

Job said, "I have not departed from the commandment of His lips; I have treasured the words of His mouth more than my necessary food" (Job 23:12). This was Job's way of saying, "When I pull myself aside to be with You, when I choose solitude, I do it because I treasure Your words more than the food that keeps me alive." David said it like this: "I made haste, and did not delay to keep Your commandments" (Ps. 119:60). Your Word is what I desire.

You see, individuals who seclude themselves become very negative, pondering the things of life they don't like or the things they don't have. But people who pull aside because they have chosen solitary refinement are those who treasure the words of God's mouth more than their necessary food. I've experienced times when my life looked like it was finished. It looked like the pressures of life were more than I could bear, when I've thought maybe I was going down for the last time.

I'll never forget when I took back-to-back trips to Asia and was prepared to go for a third. When I arrived home from the second trip, my life was turned upside down. Every fear I had been delivered from, every bit of panic in my life that I thought was part of my yesterday, came home to roost and wasn't leaving. I couldn't explain what I was facing, and I didn't know how to confront the great challenges inside my mind. I called other men of God and close friends to pray and stand in the gap for me. I sought each one's counsel, but no one could help me. Discouraged and alone, I was uncertain as to how I was going to ever make it through.

As panic struck again, my legs grew weaker. I paced the floor of our home's lower level, not wanting to let my wife, Linda, know what I was facing. I knew I wasn't the only person facing problems, but I also knew a number of people whose faith would not only waiver but whose faith might not make it at all if I failed. So I began searching my mind and scrutinizing my life, readily relying upon the only thing I knew: *If the world is going to have tribulations today, it is going to have them without me because I am making a pit stop. I'm changing my tires. I'm getting my oil changed and checking to make certain that I'll be able to run my best. I'm confessing the Word of God.*

Sometimes nothing else will do. Why did I face such a desperate struggle? I faced that struggle because I didn't change my tires as soon as I should have. I tried to take another lap. I thought, *I can get to it later and still survive*, but I went one trip too many. Sometimes you just can't take that extra lap; you must be cognizant of your own capabilities and your own limitations. Some of us maintain some very inflated feelings about who we are while others, like me, don't feel that positive about ourselves. I am not attempting to appear humble, but I truthfully don't think very highly of myself. I know who I was without Christ, and I realize that I am nothing, and can do nothing, without His grace working in my life.

You must make a decision to depend upon God for strength not only to fight but to win just as well. When you are backed into a corner and become thoroughly overwhelmed, get alone with God. Listen to the following inspiring story:

In February 2003, I learned I was pregnant. My husband and I were so excited. Everything was going well when suddenly we were dropped into hell.

We received news that my mother-in-law was in the hospital with a brain aneurysm. She was on life support for one week. She died June 28, 2003. We were devastated.

Thirty days later, my brother called and told me his fiancée's sixteen-year-old daughter and her schoolmate were killed in a car accident. The funeral was the largest I had ever been to.

Near the end of September 2003, I began having excruciating pain in my ribs. The doctors told me it was a pulled muscle or the baby was pushing at my ribs. I finally told my husband I couldn't bear the pain any longer. We went to the hospital on October 1. It turned out I had toxemia and I had to have an emergency C-section. Had I waited any longer, both my son and I would have died.

Daniel wouldn't eat from me or from a bottle. He was put in

the nursery so they could find out why he wouldn't eat. While he was in the nursery, the doctor discovered something was wrong with Daniel's heart. We soon found out that Daniel had a narrowing of his aorta, a bicuspid valve instead of a tricuspid valve (which means two flaps open to let the blood flow to the rest of the body instead of three), and a large hole in his heart. By the time Daniel was six months old, he had undergone three heart surgeries, the third one being open-heart bypass surgery. He was in the hospital a total of thirty-nine days.

Shortly after Daniel's last surgery in March 2004, my very best friend, who was like a second mother to me, died of pancreatic cancer. My husband's grandma died a few days after that. In December 2004, my friend and karate instructor was killed by a drunk driver. His was the second-largest funeral I have ever been to.

All of this happened in a very short period of time. I know that if I had not spent time with God on a regular, daily basis prior to all this happening, I would have been destroyed. Early on in my life, I read my Bible and I was always talking to God. If I didn't have the energy to open my mouth, I would write to Him. Many nights I would cry and write out my pain.

I didn't have a church home or support from anyone except my mom, my husband, and some family members. The fact that I was overwhelmed is an understatement. The devil was constantly bombarding my mind with grief, hopelessness, despair, confusion, depression, and oppression. My flesh wanted to give up and give in. It would have been easier to just give up and die. But the Greater One lives in me! I chose to live. I chose to hold on to the promises of God. And praise God I did!

For all I had lost God replaced. I now have a church home

where I am spiritually fed. I have a whole new set of friends who are on fire for God and encourage me and help push me to grow into a better individual. I am not alone anymore. That is what you get for spending time with God.

This is an exceedingly condensed version of the last four years. In order to survive these tragic deaths and my son's numerous health crises, when I wasn't dealing with matters at hand, all I desired was to be alone with God.

All that alone time I spent with God gave me strength to move on, to go on with my life even if it was an inch a day. When all of this was happening I had peace, and I completely trusted in God. I had no fear. I had a great deal of grief, pain, and heartache, but now I am stronger and tougher and so much more resilient. The devil knocked me down, but he kept forgetting that the Greater One is alive and well inside of me! I am here, I am alive, I am whole and complete. Even more important, my son is nearly four years old with a clean bill of health. Praise the Lord!

Choose solitude in the face of seclusion, every time.

—⁂—

Alone with God, Paul wrote the book of Ephesians while in prison; in Philippians 2, while alone with God, the apostle wrote of doing all things without complaining; and in Colossians 3, alone with God, the Lord's words were revealed to Paul as he wrote of "putting off the old man."

chapter seventeen

LEADING THE LINE

Devoid of her husband, her children, anyone—the woman I beheld was attending church completely alone. I pondered various scenarios that may have brought the lady to this point. Perhaps she had married a man who was unmotivated, uncommitted, or even an unbeliever, but the moment arrived when she was no longer interested in what was going to happen to him or her children; the marked moment came when her sole interest was what she needed to do in order to prevent her own life from failing.

I also had a decision to make—no longer would I allow failure to reign in my life. In a single moment, I encapsulated every bit of failure that I possibly could and steadfastly endured the pain of it. Upon doing this, I quickly began to realize how to rebuild my life out of chaos and total destruction. What began in one moment of time soon became a process that changed my whole life.

What did this process look like? Much like what you would do if you were about to upgrade a room in your home. Like striping off worn wallpaper, tearing up frayed carpeting, or replacing nicked countertops, I dismantled my life, focusing on one particular area and then attacking it forcefully with God's Word. I captured troublesome thoughts and on a daily basis purposely replaced those thoughts, using my mouth to imprint God's Word on my heart.

How did I do it? How does a person face his fears and not care what will happen next? How can you deal with the issues of life and refuse to yield to excuses?

I did those things by giving God first place in my life, by setting straight my priorities. His Word was number one, as I allowed nothing to replace my time spent with God and His Word. Now I do nothing without first knowing it will please God in the end. Putting God first doesn't merely mean praying the moment you wake up; it entails an entire lifestyle that pleases God.

The apostle John instructed, "Little children, keep yourselves from idols (false gods)—[from anything and everything that would occupy the place in your heart due to God, from any sort of substitute for Him that would take first place in your life]" (1 John 5:21 AMP). Jesus taught, "Seek (aim at and strive after) first of all His kingdom and His righteousness (His way of doing and being right), and then all these things taken together [what you eat, drink, and wear] will be given you besides" (Matt. 6:33 AMP).

Why not begin to approach everything in life by order of priority? Never determine your priorities by what you want, by your problems, or by the pressures you're feeling. Determine today that your number one objective is to do what is right. Discovering what is right can only be accomplished through diligent study of God's Word and knowing His heart. Setting priorities places certain boundaries and various safeguards around your life, always keeping you aimed in the right direction. Establishing the right priorities protects you from becoming dubious about what is true and what is false, what's important and what's not important.

I remember when I wanted to witness to a couple who took care of Linda while I was in the mental institution. I didn't know how to witness except to convey my testimony to them. This couple had been so kind to Linda; the husband was a great guy, had a great job, and had his act together. So one day I told the man I wanted to get together with him.

He said to me, "Can we get together on Sunday?"

Quickly I replied, "I'm sorry, I can't get together on Sunday."

He answered, "Well, how about Sunday night?"

I said, "No, no . . ."

He then said, "I thought you wanted to talk to me?"

I said, "I really do."

"But you can't get together on Sunday?"

"No, how about Monday?" I managed.

"I'll be out of town Monday and Tuesday," he responded. "How about Wednesday?"

"Sorry, I can't get together with you on Wednesday. How about Thursday?"

He said, "No, I'll be out of town again. How about Sunday?"

I said, "Sorry, I can't get together Sunday morning or Sunday night."

Then he reiterated, "I thought you wanted to talk to me."

I said, "I do!" And finally I did, but only after sticking to my priorities. I was committed to going to church on Sundays and Wednesday evenings, and I had to arrange my schedule around those commitments, even when it was difficult or inconvenient.

Priority simply means greatest importance. What's most important to *you?*

People try to build a life in the midst of the hustle and bustle of our muddled society. They are so busy that after a little while they begin to blame God for their busyness, even though God didn't have anything to do with the way they set their schedules. People overcrowd their lives when they add too many things over and above their priorities. Finally, their worldly commitments scream so loudly their godly commitments give in.

It's easy to give up godly commitments because God is the only one who won't speak up about it. Just like a cell phone call that gets dropped or the signal becomes fuzzy, in life the same thing is true; the signal between God and us can weaken. We no longer are sensitive to His leading and His guiding. It is at this place that we must repent and turn toward God. Only then can God help us reset our priorities and truly live for Him.

What happened? Why did the signal fade? "They are the ones who hear the word, and the cares of this world, the deceitfulness of riches, and the desires for other things entering in choke the word, and it becomes unfruitful" (Mark 4:18–19). The things that choke the Word in our lives are anxieties, distractions, the false glamour of riches, and the craving for other things. These are the very viruses that attack the Word in your life, causing you to fail. Surprisingly, these worries and pleasures don't choke *you*; instead, they choke the Word of God, which is the only source of strength and power to live a victorious life.

Satan desires to neutralize you. Be alert, because when the devil can't steal the Word from you by sending bad things your way, he will try to steal it by distracting you with good things. Some may say, "Everything's great, my business is strong, everything's wonderful, but oh gosh, I have to work again tonight. I'm sorry I won't have time for God tonight, but the Lord understands. God knows exactly what I'm going through, and besides, He's the one who gave me this business." People tend to think, *if He's the one who gave me this business, He must be the one who wants me to blow off my responsibilities.*

If I desire to render your life ineffective, I don't need to hurt you and I don't need to destroy your family. All I need to do is distract you from your priorities. If I succeed in neutralizing you, you can still go to church and discreetly *appear* as though God is still number one in your life. In reality, you'll only be an example of a person who lost his commitment to God but still looks like he's blessed. This is how many people live. They live uncommitted lives yet attempt to appear godly.

In order to establish right priorities, however, you must first be willing to get alone. Each of us must pull aside from our busy and self-indulgent schedules. Then, in order to keep our priorities, we must alter our normal state of affairs on a consistent basis. That means scheduling time for ourselves and making a priority of keeping that commitment.

So I have listed a few priorities that must be established in your life.

PRIORITY #1: INVEST TIME ALONE WITH GOD EVERY MORNING

Can you think of a better way to jump-start your day? Even when you don't wake up on the proverbial right side of the bed, you can start on the right foot by first being alone with God. When you set aside time alone with God early in the morning, you'll be following the example of many great men and women who have gone before you. Scriptures speak of times when godly people such as David, Hannah, Moses, and Job met God in the morning. Mark 1:35 reports a time when Jesus arose before dawn to pray in a solitary place.

In an interview with *Reader's Digest*, Billy Graham revealed, "Almost since the night I accepted Jesus Christ into my life as a teenager, I have tried to set aside time each morning to be alone with God. This time includes prayer, reading the Bible, and meditating on its meaning. Nothing has been more important to my spiritual life."[1]

Don't look at anything until you've met this first priority. Don't read the newspaper until you've first read the Bible. Don't consult your computer before you first consult God. If you prioritize alone-time with God, all other priorities will inevitably fall into line.

Over time, I've recognized moments in my life when God began to move deeply inside me, manifesting Himself *in* me, not just *to* me. Some years ago while working as a meat cutter, I'll never forget meeting the wife of pastor and author A. W. Tozer. There I was at work, where I admit that I cut my own skin more often than I cut the meat, when she walked in and said, "I'm Mrs. A. W. Tozer." I immediately sensed the presence of God in her life. Interestingly, A. W. Tozer was the man who said, "It is important that we get still to wait on God and it's the best that we get alone, preferably with our Bible outspread before us. Then if we will, we may draw near to God and begin to hear Him speak to us in our hearts."[2]

This is what I seek after with my entire being every day: "God, I want to know You. I want to know Your words. I want to know how You feel about things. God, I want more of Your presence." Unless I'm able to manifest His glory to others, what would be the far-reaching good in being alone with Him?

A businessman shares:

In my line of business, I have the opportunity to travel locally in my vehicle most of the day. This enables me to start my day with praise and worship, and then move on to a teaching tape or CD. I have listened to some of these over fifty times, gaining new insights each time. This allows me to go into the workplace and use what I have been meditating on over and over again. Recently I have been able to share with others what I have learned from this, and it has been timely information to help minister to others.

My alone-time in the Word every day enables me to build a foundation of the Word of God in my life, and it comes out in my actions in the workplace. By keeping my word, being organized, solving problems for others, and having an excellent attitude, I am applying the teachings from the Word of God every day in the workplace.

When you spend time alone with God, His Word will become alive. What once was boring will become vibrant and fresh. The words on the pages will infuse you with God's power to perform His work and obey His Word. When God's Word comes alive, there is only one thing that can stop you: neglect of getting alone and spending more quality time in His Word.

Commit to "be strong in the Lord [be empowered through your union with Him]" (Eph. 6:10 AMP).

PRIORITY #2: PRAY FOR AUTHORITY

If you expect to go anywhere with God, you need to love those whom God has put in charge because your loyalty is not to humanity, your loyalty is only to God. "I exhort *first of all* that supplications, prayers, intercessions, and giving of thanks be made for all men, for kings and all who are in authority, that we may lead a quiet and peaceable life in all godliness and reverence" (1 Tim. 2:1–2; emphasis added).

In America, we live in a generation that despises authority. Our nation was birthed in rebellion; therefore, rebellion is part of our nature. But God says, "Look, I want you to pray for people in authority. I don't want you resisting all the time, because you not only resist praying for the bad ones, you also resist praying for the good ones."

The reason you pray for the president is so you may lead a quiet and peaceable life in the Lord. Our land is filled with turmoil, so pray for those in authority. In Ezra 6:10, King Darius issued a decree that a governor named Tattenai should allow the Jews to build the house of God and to "offer sacrifices of sweet aroma to the God of heaven, and pray for the life of the king and his sons." Therefore, pray for the lives of those in government. Whether you realize it or not, disagreement never got you anything from the very first time you said no. Rebellion didn't work for you then, and it doesn't work for you now. Pleasing God means praying for and submitting to those in positions of authority.

Submission is the willingness to bow your knee before men in order to satisfy the requirements of heaven. We bow our knees before men to please heaven and not to please men. I'm going to please heaven, regardless. If you're an authority in my life, I will submit myself to you because I will submit to heaven.

PRIORITY #3: MEDITATE ON GOD'S WORD

If you're going to think anything, think what God thinks. People tend to spend a lot of time thinking about clothing and food, but what in the world do a new suit and hot apple pie have over Jesus?

When Jesus came into the coasts of a region called Caesarea Philippi, He asked His disciples, "Who do men say that I, the Son of Man, am?" (Matt. 16:13). One by one, they began to speak up. One person said, "Some say you're Elijah." Another one declared, "You're one of the prophets." So Jesus asked, "But who do you say that I am?" (v. 15). Then Peter proclaimed, "You are the Christ, the Son of the living God" (v. 16). That was the answer Jesus was seeking. What man could have unraveled all that yarn? Who could have unlocked that safe? Jesus responded to Peter, "Blessed are you, Simon Bar-Jonah, for flesh and blood has not revealed this to you, but My Father who is in heaven" (v. 17).

You see, even though one man knew the answer, not everybody knew it. David prayed, "Open my eyes, that I may see wondrous things from Your law" (Ps. 119:18). David was praying, "God, open my eyes so I can see what You are saying, not just read words on a parchment. I need to have my eyes opened."

You could tell me every spiritual thing you know, and even though I would want to understand with all of my heart, I couldn't understand until I was personally willing to search it out for myself. What may be revelation to me can be information to the person I share it with. Meditation will cause information to become revelation.

The apostle Paul prayed for us in this way: "I keep asking that the God of our Lord Jesus Christ, the glorious Father, may give you the Spirit of wisdom and revelation, so that you may know him better"

(Eph. 1:17 NIV). The mystery of "Christ in us" begins to unravel in the alone moment when we choose to get to know Him better.

Who is He? I need to know who He is, not just hear about Him. I need to know Him, not only about the kind of things He once did. I need to know what He wants to do today. What is He interested in doing in my life? What is He interested in doing in your life? We can know these things by intently meditating upon the Word of God.

The same way rain falls to earth and soaks the parched soil causing flowers to grow, God's Word falls from heaven onto the soft soil of my heart, causing growth in things that appear dead. "As the rain and the snow come down from heaven, and do not return to it without watering the earth and making it bud and flourish . . . so is my word that goes out from my mouth: It will not return to me empty, but will accomplish what I desire and achieve the purpose for which I sent it" (Isa. 55:10–11 NIV).

The psalmist exclaimed, "Oh, how I love your law! I meditate on it all day long" (Ps. 119:97 NIV). Is this your heart's cry? "All day long, Your Word is what I think about. All day, I want to know You, to fellowship with You, to know how You want things done."

PRIORITY #4: CONFESS GOD'S WORD

You can't rid your mind of negative thoughts by repeatedly thinking, *I don't want to think those thoughts. I'm not going to think those thoughts anymore. Those thoughts aren't my thoughts. Those aren't my thoughts, in Jesus' name.*

The moment you began to open your mouth, other thoughts abruptly stopped. Likewise, when you are confessing God's Word, you are halting the internal voices. Negative thoughts that bombard you are not a part of you; they sneak in from the outside. To counter-act them, bombard your mind with scriptures that stop other thoughts from speaking. As you meditate upon these scriptures, start to confess them out loud. However, do not confess scriptures against a problem. Instead of focusing on your problem, focus on God's transforming Word. You will always move in the direction of your focus.

Speak of future events with as much guarantee as if they were already in the past. Why can you do that? Because God Himself "speaks of future events with as much certainty as though they were already past" (Rom. 4:17 TLB).

Don't you get tired of praying about problems? Begin to cement this concept into your thought patterns: *my problem is already behind me.* The thoughts running through your mind are nothing more than renegades of the past looking up an old friend. They are fugitives that escaped from the yesterdays of your life that plague your mind.

Negative thoughts are nothing more than distracting thoughts. Distraction ultimately equals destruction. If you can be distracted, you can be destroyed. How many times have people been distracted by their cell phones and ended up in car accidents? How many times have you heard people say, "I didn't know it was about to happen, and it happened so quickly"? That's because they were distracted. Negative thoughts are only there to do one thing—confuse you to the point where you're so old you die before getting free through con-fessing the Word.

You can transform an area of your life by meditating on and con-fessing two or three scriptures. When you confess the Word of God, you only need to take two or three scriptures for each area you want to change. This is a manageable amount, enabling you to be able to confess them daily. When you confess, you declare your faith. Take one of the areas you desire to be changed and declare your faith through corresponding scriptures for an entire week.

At one point in my life, I was so sick I thought I was going to die. I kept confessing Romans 8:11: "But if the Spirit of him that raised up Jesus from the dead dwell in you, he that raised up Christ from the dead shall also quicken your mortal bodies by his Spirit that dwelleth in you" (KJV). So I would say, "Jesus, the same Spirit who raised Christ from the dead lives in me, and He who raised Christ from the dead has brought to my whole being, yes, even to my mortal body new strength and vitality. Jesus, I just want to thank You that the same Spirit who raised You from the dead dwells inside me, and because He dwells inside me, You'll give strength to my mortal body."

God said to me, *What have you been saying with your mouth?*

Thinking He was rebuking me, I replied, "But, Lord, I've been saying what You have said about me."

This was His response: *Then get up!*

I jumped up, danced down the stairs, and worshiped God as I drove to work because the same Spirit who raised Christ from the dead lives in me. If He lives in me, He's given strength to my mortal body. He's given me new strength and vitality because He lives inside me!

For instance, if you are experiencing failure in your life, take a look at 2 Corinthians 2:14, which says, "Now thanks be to God who always leads us in triumph in Christ." Therefore you can say, "Father, I thank You because You lead me in one continual triumph in Christ. Father, I thank You for leading me from victory to victory."

First Corinthians 15:57 says, "But thanks be to God, who gives us the victory through our Lord Jesus Christ." Therefore I say, "Father, I want to thank You that You have given me the victory through my Lord and Savior Jesus Christ. I'm not trying to become victorious; I already am victorious because You have given me the victory. Victory is already mine. I already have it."

I'm not going to sit around the house or the office bummed out over the idea that I'm trying to get victory. Jesus says I *have* the victory. If He says it, then I believe it. I would even add to my arsenal of confessions the verse that says, "For whatever is born of God overcomes the world. And this is the victory that has overcome the world—our faith" (1 John 5:4). So I say, "Father, I thank You that I am born of God and I've overcome the world. And this is the victory that overcomes the world, my faith."

I have discovered something that has made the pivotal difference in my life and that is setting my priorities straight. When you and I set our priorities straight, everything falls into place. Invest time alone with God every morning, pray for those in authority, and meditate on and confess God's Word.

Remember, "by giving himself completely at the Cross, actually dying for you, Christ brought you over to God's side and put your lives together, whole and holy in his presence. *You stay grounded and steady in that bond of trust, constantly tuned in to the Message, careful not to be distracted or diverted.*

Let's continually allow Him to "lead the line" of everything and everyone else inside our busy lives, making Him priority number one.

—⁂—

In I Thessalonians 2, alone with God, the apostle Paul wrote about enduring persecution, and in 2 Thessalonians 3, after being alone with God, Paul encouraged his brothers in the Lord not to be weary in doing good. In 1 Timothy 2, alone with God, Paul proclaimed that there is one Mediator between God and men, the Man Christ Jesus; in 2 Timothy 3, also alone with God, Paul shared how people will act in the perilous last days.

chapter eighteen

WONDROUSLY WILLING

How long have you been a believer? Thirty days? Three months? Several decades? I've been a Christian for more than thirty years, and I've observed that over time, things begin to slip, whether we admit it or not. As they begin to slip, we begin to take some things for granted. We begin to ask, "What can I get from this relationship with God?" We no longer see life from God's perspective, but our own.

As I travel the world, I discover that most airplanes and hotels aren't as glamorous as I'd heard. I hear of missionaries in the country I'm visiting being robbed and of their very lives being put at stake. I've asked myself more than once, *What in the world am I doing here? I have responsibilities at home.*

Most of us remember that fateful day in 1999 when Cassie Bernall, a Columbine High School student, was asked if she believed in God. When she answered with a resounding "Yes," she was shot dead. We tend to think there is no cost to believing in God, but how can we forget what happened to the disciples who walked with Jesus?

According to Acts 12, King Herod Agrippa had the apostle James killed with a sword. The apostle Peter was crucified upside down on an X-shaped cross in Rome, which fulfilled Jesus' prophecy in John 21. Killed by a sword, Matthew suffered martyrdom in Ethiopia. During a wave of persecution in Rome, John faced martyrdom when he was thrown into a huge basin of boiling oil. He was miraculously delivered from death but then sentenced to work the mines on the prison island of Patmos. James, the half brother of Jesus and leader of the church in Jerusalem, was thrown more than one hundred feet down from the southeast pinnacle of the temple after he refused to deny his faith in Christ. When his persecutors discovered he survived the fall, they beat James to death with a club. By the way, this was the same pinnacle where Satan tempted Jesus to bow down in exchange for the whole world.

Bartholomew, also known as Nathanael, was a missionary to Asia. He witnessed in present-day Turkey and was martyred for his preaching in Armenia. In Greece, after being whipped severely by seven soldiers, Andrew's body was tied with cords to an X-shaped cross to prolong his agony. He continued to preach to his tormentors for two days until he finally passed away. The apostle Thomas was stabbed with a spear in India during one of his missionary trips to establish a church. Matthias, the apostle chosen to replace the traitor Judas Iscariot, was stoned and then beheaded. The apostle Paul was tortured and subsequently beheaded by the evil emperor Nero at Rome in AD 67.

The courage to face these fateful moments is forged only when you are alone, not when you're in a crowd. Boldness doesn't surface when everyone's raising their hands and getting excited, running, jumping, shouting, and praising God. Fateful moments are only embraced when you have cultivated the internal strength to truthfully say, "Death, where is your sting? Grave, where is your victory?"

I long for the day when I would be deemed worthy to be put to death for the name of Christ. I pray that you will be like-minded.

TO WALK WITH GOD, YOU MUST SURRENDER TO GOD

When you hold a pen in your hand, the pen is completely surrendered to your desired use of it. When I put on a jacket, the jacket surrenders to my form. I well remember the day, almost thirty-one years ago, when I surrendered my life to God. It wasn't that I didn't believe in God already, but I hadn't surrendered to Him. Back and forth, from the time when I was six, I believed in God. But I had had an intermittent relationship with Him, never truly knowing Him until the moment I surrendered.

Most people you know keep one foot in the church and the other in the world. Does the Bible say anyone who walked with Jesus behaved that way? Of course not. There is currently a doctrine in the church called universalism. Universalism erroneously states that Satan and Judas will walk down the streets of gold together because of ultimate forgiveness. But when people don't want to surrender, they create new doctrines that are nothing more than what the Bible calls "doctrines of demons" (1 Tim. 4:1).

We spend so much time teaching people about dreams and

visions, yet we have less accomplishment than ever. We've created spiritual teenagers. Spiritual teenagers are always excited that demons are subject to the name of Jesus. Instead of discovering what God wants them to do, they're always telling you what *they* want to do. Most of the time they want to become a success, not realizing that true success is becoming who God has created them to be. Becoming who God created you to be means surrendering your own feelings, your individual dreams, everything you want to the point where they don't matter anymore and saying, "Lord, not as I will but as You will."

Mark 8:34 says, "When [Jesus] had called the people to Himself, with His disciples also, He said to them, 'Whoever desires to come after Me, let him deny himself, and take up his cross, and follow Me.'" Will you walk with Jesus?

It is foolish to believe that you can walk with God and not do what He says. God doesn't work with people who don't obey Him. The minute you resign yourself, the moment you surrender your will, is the moment you find out God's. So I ask you, how much are you really surrendering? Up to what you think is safe? Pleasing Jesus doesn't work that way. God is able to protect you, but what He really wants is your surrender.

Of Enoch, Genesis 5 records, "Enoch lived 365 years, walking in close fellowship with God. Then one day he disappeared, because God took him" (vv. 23–24 NLT).

Of Noah, Genesis 6 accounts, "Noah was a righteous man, the only blameless person living on earth at the time, and he walked in close fellowship with God" (v. 9 NLT).

Of Himself, Jesus said, "He who sent Me is with Me . . . for I always do those things that please Him" (John 8:29).

The overwhelming reason for spending time with God is to be

transformed, to think and to act like Him, not to get something you want. I only know a few people who do this, people who, when push comes to shove, always say and do what God says. Most people are simply nice people who only transform about a quarter-inch deep but who become vengeful when they're angry and upset.

Over a hundred years ago, pastor Andrew Murray said, "I am sure there are Christians who long for the higher life and who sometimes have received a great blessing. I am sure that there are those who have, at times, found a great inflow of heavenly joy and a great outflow of heavenly gladness. Yet, after a time, it passes away. They've not understood that close, personal communication with Christ is an absolute necessity for daily life. Take time to be alone with Christ. Nothing in heaven or in earth can free you from the necessity for this if you are to be committed to being a holy Christian."

I would have thought that the apostle Paul would have grabbed every mentor he could find when he came to Christ. But the Bible says something completely different. It doesn't record that Paul pushed anyone away, but it does state that he withdrew for seventeen years. Before he could preach to the public, he had to privately know who God was within him. In Galatians 1:15–16, he reveals, "When it pleased God, who separated me from my mother's womb and called me through His grace, to reveal His Son in me, that I might preach Him among the Gentiles, I did not immediately confer with flesh and blood."

You see, Jesus cannot exalt you publicly until He first mentors you privately. Entering into a time alone may feel scary, but there's nothing more exciting than privacy with Jesus. Matthew 6:6 instructs, "When you pray, go into your room, and when you have shut your door, pray to your Father who is in the secret place; and your Father who sees in secret will reward you openly."

David said, "One thing I have desired of the LORD, that will I seek: That I may dwell in the house of the LORD all the days of my life, to behold the beauty of the LORD, and to inquire in His temple" (Ps. 27:4).

David desired only one thing. What one thing are you running after?

TO LIVE BY HEAVEN'S WAYS MEANS YOU'LL OFTEN WALK ALONE

If you're going to live life by heaven's directives, most often you'll walk alone. If you ever find someone to walk beside you, never let him go because he's a rare find. Which are you more committed to: God's Word or the opinion of man? Sad to say, I believe most people are more interested in men's opinions than God's words. They wrongly believe that men's opinions are on equal footing with God's Word. God's Word is all we have, all we must live for, and all we must be willing to die for. If you desire to live by heaven's ways, you will often walk alone; many people you know won't choose to walk the same path and will think you're an oddity.

I'll never forget the first time I faced some rejection because I surrendered my marriage to the Lord. My fellow employees couldn't handle seeing me leave work with a dress for Linda in one arm and flowers for her in the other. They constantly made cutting remarks and jokes. They wouldn't let it go, every day. Every moment they had a chance, they would tear me down with their words. They also despised me because I worked harder and faster than they ever did. You see, when you serve the Lord Jesus Christ, you work for God instead of the company, and your boss receives the benefit.

As a brand-new believer, I remember experiencing rejection among fellow church members. In one church I attended, the men would attend a Men's Steak Fry. We would ride a bus to camp, spend the night, and eat a lot of steak.

On the bus, a man who sat in the back yelled to me in the front, saying, "Hey, Thompson, God show you anything today?" This man happened to be the person everyone considered as the most on fire for God, so the whole bus erupted in laughter at me. Incidentally, these were the same men who held Bible contests. As a new Christian, I couldn't figure out why I knew where various scriptures were located and what they meant, when none of the other men did. They'd been saved for much longer, so I couldn't figure out why they didn't know every page of the Bible!

It's difficult to discuss the Word with Christians who argue about its meaning; many would rather fight to bring you captive to their unbelief than completely surrender to the Lord. But don't yield to them; understand that you will become a trophy to hell the moment you surrender to unbelief. If you really want to obey God's Word, you're going to have to do it alone for a season. If you're looking for a whole busload of people to support your faith in Christ, you might as well forget it. Facing rejection is part of living for Jesus, to which Paul referred when he prayed about the "fellowship of His sufferings" (Phil. 3:10).

I often wondered why Isaiah 40:31 referred to eagles. But then I learned that when these majestic birds molt, they shed all of their feathers, causing them to become extremely vulnerable. Without feathers, they are unable to fly away from danger. To protect themselves, they soar to the highest rock they can find before their feathers fall out. All by themselves, huddled on the towering rock, they lie in the sun and wait. Interestingly, eagles fly to a safe place where they will lose their ability to fly. Even so, they trust they will fly again. Similarly, if we're serious about our walk with God, we must be willing to give it all up so we can get it all back with Him again. How serious are you? How much of your own feelings and your own desires are you willing to give up so you can be what He wants you to be? Or are you the kind of person who wants to go halfway just to get what you want?

Recently I was talking to a young lady who was in the middle of a divorce. I said, "Sweetie, you know one of the things people never notice?"

She said, "What's that?"

"You will never have the grace in your thirties that God gave to you in your twenties because God is expecting you to be different in your thirties than you were in your twenties. He's expecting you to walk closer to Him in your forties than you did in your thirties. He's expecting you to walk more with Him in your fifties than you ever did in your forties. He's expecting you to prepare for the end because it may all be required of you one day. What do you want? Do you want what you've got or do you want what *He* offers?"

After teaching in a synagogue one day, Jesus' disciples discussed His words and complained, "Now, wait a minute. What does this mean? For three and a half years we've walked with You and now You're saying to do this?" From that moment forward, many of His disciples "walked with Him no more" (John 6:66).

How devastating it must have felt for people to leave Him, people into whom Jesus had poured His life. I wonder if He had to silence a voice that whispered, *Your life has been a waste!* And to make matters worse, later one of His closest friends, the apostle Peter, left Him and lied about ever having known Him.

Despite this rejection, Jesus was wondrously willing as He obediently went to the cross. And when He did, *He went alone*. You see, to live life by heaven's ways often means you'll walk alone. When Peter denied knowing Jesus, he hadn't yet understood the cost of walking alone. I can tell you that if you're ever going to walk alone, you have to be willing to lose it all every second of every day. So let's continually be wondrously willing.

—⚊—

In Titus 1, alone with God, Paul revealed the spiritual guidelines for overseers, and in the tiny book of Philemon, alone with God, Paul encouraged his young convert, Onesimus. In Hebrews 11, alone with God, the apostle exhorted Christians to live faith-filled lives.

chapter nineteen

GUARANTEED GREATNESS

Like a car stranded without gas in the wilderness, before I came to Jesus, my life was going nowhere. Frankly, it was over. Although only in my early twenties, life seemed to be approaching its final act. The sad part was, I had no desire to live. If you want to live, that's one thing; but life sinks to a terrible, disappointing low when you experience enough of being a loser that you want to lose your life as well. I felt I deserved to lose. I can't explain the level of rejection and soul-wrenching disappointment I suffered beginning at an early age. I could have chosen to live the rest of my life with a victim mentality, as rejected people typically do. Yet, instead of living under the thumb of rejection, I decided not to pay the price of disappointment for the rest of my life, since harboring blame is way too costly. I gave up blaming others for a close, ongoing relationship with Jesus.

A town prostitute once visited Jesus to repent of her sins. The fact that Jesus was eating dinner with a man who disapproved of her did nothing to break her resolve. In the presence of rejection, this woman utterly humbled herself by weeping all over Jesus' feet and then kneeling to dry them with her own hair. She finished her sacrificial presentation by massaging a very expensive bottle of perfumed oil into His feet. What was the end result of this woman's actions? Jesus forgave her sins and gave her peace from the distresses her sins had caused (Luke 7:36–50).

At what expense did this prostitute press through the crowd in order to see Jesus? I'm sure more than just one man ridiculed her along the way, trying to keep her away from Him. Yet through her tears she pressed through the tangled mass of humanity. And through her tears she refused to give up. Through her tears she made certain to contact Jesus face-to-face.

Can you imagine how it must have felt to be liberated from her sinful lifestyle? Can you imagine her joy of entering into a life filled with love? And yet this newfound love and freedom wouldn't have occurred if she hadn't pressed through.

Just like this woman, I experienced, and am still carving, a transformed life.

Isn't time a fascinating device to observe? Time marches on, whether we want it to or not. When we were young, we tried to will the hands on the clock to move ahead. But when we grew a little older, we tried to make the clock stop. Jim Croce sang, "If I could save time in a bottle."[1] We try to do whatever we can to eliminate the pain, to eradicate the ugliness that encroaches over time. In one sense, time seems so rewarding. But if we were to investigate it truthfully, we would see the unkind beat to which it marches. Day after day, it seems to say, the consequences of everything in which we have indulged are steadily approaching. We can't stop penalties from reaching us with its compass of righteousness.

Nonetheless, I found something that could powerfully change things, something that actually works. In the Bible, I don't ever find Jesus talking to people about someone else. No, I always find Him talking to people straight up about themselves. Inside of that, I discovered something even more powerful: these were people who were willing to be transparent. These were people who were willing to allow Jesus to glimpse into their hearts, to cut and paste, as well as penetrate their minds. These were people who would admit, "Jesus, I was wrong."

Do you think the woman who poured the perfumed oil on Jesus felt for even one moment that she was sinless? She sobbed because she knew she was wrong; she mourned the wasted years with a willingness to reach into a new future. This willingness to reach toward a better tomorrow is what changes the unkind beat of time to one of promise for a brighter future. This, my friends, is the essence of the gospel. The essence of the gospel is not "Oh don't worry about it." The gospel is "Let's get real today, and tomorrow will wipe wrong away." Even though God extends His mercy to sinners, sin matters greatly to Him. The mercy of God says, "Even though sin has taken such a great toll on you, I will fix it. I'll make the rough places plain. I'll take your broken life and mend it back together. No matter what you've experienced, I'll make you better. All you must do is repent and believe upon Jesus." That's the gospel.

God wants you to deal with your issues. He'll make you better.

He'll work with you through the pain, the shame, the fear, and the disappointment. But it won't happen by listening to the crowd. Being alone doesn't necessarily mean being without anyone in a room. Being alone means that for the moment, others' thoughts and sentiments are of no account; right now, the only thing that matters is what heaven thinks. When a person yields his life to God in his alone moments, he doesn't know where God will lead him along the journey. He's uncertain about where God will take him, and lives risking all aspects of his life to God. But somehow, in some way, he feels attached to a divine string that is suspending him above destruction.

GREATNESS COMES TO THOSE WHO CHOOSE TO BE ALONE WITH GOD

Greatness comes to us in allowing ourselves to approach heaven and then allowing heaven to radiate within us; allowing the radiation of eternity to invade our humanity. After Moses had been alone with God on a mountain, his face radiated with the presence of God (Ex. 34:29).

One time when I was disciplining my son, he began to negotiate with me about his spanking. I explained, "Now here's what's going to happen. You're going to catch this twice, so don't put your hands where I can hurt them."

He protested, "No, not twice! Only once."

He expected me to say, "That'll be fine," but instead I said, "No. Twice."

He whined, "No, Dad! Just once."

I said, "Okay, son. Three times."

We act the same way when we go to God with a problem. We have a thorn in our paw, but we're telling God, "Don't touch the thorn. You can give me a manicure, but don't touch the thorn because it's sore."

But God says, "Now look, it's infected. I have to go in there to remove it and clean you up. Hold still—this is going to hurt." Have you ever read and wondered about the verse that says "*If need be*, you have been grieved by various trials" (1 Pet. 1:6; emphasis added)? It means if you don't surrender quickly enough, something you don't want will happen in your life.

Thus, keep submitting to God. Fight the easy spirit of self-righteousness that gloats, *I'm better than you, so I must have it made.* Am I really the standard against which you measure yourself? Funny, but I thought God *was* the standard. Being alone with God means I'm willing to stand for godliness by myself no matter what anyone else says. Being alone with God means I'm willing to become what is necessary before Him. Alone is the place where God chooses those who will be used by Him and those who will lead for Him. Who you are as a person, what your future will be, and how well you influence people is formed alone.

GREATNESS COMES TO THOSE WHO DILIGENTLY SEARCH FOR GOD

The process of diligently searching for God transforms you into a person who is great in God's eyes. The process of wanting God with everything you are transforms you into who He has called you to be. While you are undertaking that process, you are unknowingly becoming great in God's eyes.

Demon spirits have voices. Listening to their voices has kept some people from becoming great in God's eyes. People have listened to the voices of demons and consequently have made wrong choices. Sadly, people have blamed God for these choices. We tend to think that we are not affected by our surroundings. Take a look at nature—fish flourish in water, but when you remove them from their aquatic environment, they can't breathe very well. People are healthy living out of the water, but if you leave us in the water too long, we drown. Please understand, there is a place where you will do well and there is a place where you won't.

Luke 5 informs us that Jesus went alone to the wilderness to pray. Galatians 1 tells us the apostle Paul spent time alone with God in Arabia and then in Damascus.

David's greatness was birthed while he was out in the field worshiping God. He spent so much time alone that he developed a confidence in God that none of his brothers could have in their crowd. When Saul offered him protective armor to face Goliath, David responded, "No, I can't trust in that. I can trust facing Goliath alone because I know the power of being alone" (1 Sam. 17:32–51). When the day came for him to face off with the giant Goliath, he was ready. Even though his brothers rejected him, he reprimanded them, loudly proclaiming, "Is there not a cause?" (1 Sam. 17:29). David faced the giant and won, delivering God's people from their enemy.

Stop trying to get your uniform fixed up before you join God's cause. The reason most things go wrong with people is because they don't share Jesus with anybody. Is it okay with you that people you know are ticking away toward death without a Savior? Without ever even wanting to, you become an undershepherd of God's sheep the moment you choose to be alone with Him. You become like Him; you think like Him and you talk like Him. Inexplicably, you become more divine than human. Even though in your humanity you groan every day wanting to go to heaven, yet at the same time you realize, *He's my father and I'm his child. I will act like my father, not like my brothers.* And at that moment, things change.

GREATNESS COMES TO THOSE WHO ANSWER HIS CALL

God calls everyone, but only those who answer His voice become great.

During King Darius's reign in Persia, some men asked him to sign a law forbidding anyone to pray for thirty days or be thrown into a den of lions. "When Daniel knew that the writing was signed, he went home. And in his upper room, with his windows open toward Jerusalem, he knelt down on his knees three times that day, and prayed and gave thanks before his God, as was his custom since early days" (Dan. 6:10). Daniel didn't change at all. Daniel's greatness came, however, as he pictured himself on God's side of the issue, not on humanity's side.

I'm not on humanity's side of the issue anymore. I no longer care about man's opinion because now I belong to God, my Father. Being alone with God helps you to become like your Father. Are you willing to stand *alone?* Are you willing to endure rejection from everyone else? You must "endure hardship as a good soldier of Jesus Christ. No one engaged in warfare entangles himself with the affairs of this life, that he may please him who enlisted him as a soldier" (2 Tim. 2:3–4). We must please the One who enlisted us.

As you spend time alone with God, He will transform you into a truly loving person; instead of being just one of the guys routinely hanging out like you always have, you will be a person with the Scriptures open, bringing your friends back to their walk with God.

What kind of person are you? Are you like Moses, or are you like his brother, Aaron? Moses was a man who always represented God, no matter what. He didn't sit on the proverbial fence, nor did he represent a person's point of view. Moses was a person who wanted to know, based on the Word of God, why you feel what you feel. And if you don't have a reason, give it up.

But Aaron listened to the people. When someone would approach him with a complaint, he was a "tell me what's bothering you" kind of a person. He would say, "Oh, I understand why you're feeling this. You're right, things shouldn't be that way." Or he'd say, "I agree with you 100 percent."

Have you ever noticed that every time people approach you with a complaint, the conversation is typically about a person for whom they work, not about someone who works for them? Criticisms are usually directed northward and rarely southward. People don't become jealous of anyone they're greater than. It's easy to criticize those who have achieved more than you, becoming offended because you didn't achieve it. The Aaron kind of people may wrap their arms around everybody, but they're the ones who are also slitting your throat behind your back. You see, the Moses kind of person truly loves you—he will tell you the truth about yourself. The Bible observes, "Faithful are the wounds of a friend" (Prov. 27:6).

When my wife needs help, the best thing I can do is tell her the truth about herself, not just say, "Oh, you're okay, baby." It's better to argue about the truth today than allow her to be tormented for years to come.

As parents, you can decide to do what's right, not according to your opinion, but according to God's, knowing that your children belong to Him, not to you. Just remember, those young people your children hang out with every day want them to do worse things than they're doing now. Don't think these issues are going to disappear—you must face off with them because they will only worsen. Children hide things from their parents; they won't tell you how many abortions they're having or that they were in a gunfight last week.

God isn't a negotiator. You can only come face-to-face with God when you stop trying to negotiate with Him. Some people take three steps forward and then fall four steps back. But "you were bought at a price; therefore glorify God in your body, and in your spirit, which are God's" (1 Cor. 6:20). If you'll decide to stand for the things of God, regardless of what anybody thinks, regardless of what anybody says, Luke 21:19 promises, "By standing firm you will gain life" (NIV).

Your future is closer than you think. Today's choices will determine your destiny and your impact on your generation. The birthplace of guaranteed greatness is the destiny of those who choose to be alone to hear God's voice.

—◊—

In James 1, James, the half brother of Jesus, while alone with God, received the encouragement that we should count trials a joy; in 1 Peter 2, the apostle Peter, alone with God, relayed that believers are a "chosen generation"; while in 2 Peter 2, alone with God, Peter warned of false prophets among God's people. In 1, 2, and 3 John, the apostle John, after being alone with God, detailed the value of love and righteousness.

chapter twenty

REFINED REFLECTIONS

s we've learned throughout this study, there is a subtle, hidden power in being alone. As Lily Tomlin once quipped, "Remember, we're all in this alone."

Thankfully, I've discovered that being alone with God is a beneficial and unending adventure. Through being alone with God, He has transformed the way I think, feel, and act. Undergoing a sense of wholeness and completeness, I concur with David, who declared, "God is . . . my portion forever" (Ps. 73:26).

Time spent alone in refined reflection with God is a must. It is something we *must* embrace, something we *must* do, something we all *must* desire. When we humble ourselves before God and take time to be with the Creator of the universe, we will never be the same. Mark

Twain once observed, "Naked people have little or no influence in society." So don't leave home without clothing yourself in humility each day (1 Pet. 5:5).

In the 1600s, William Bradford sailed the *Mayflower* to America, where he became governor of Plymouth Colony. Large parts of his handwritten journal were later published in *Of Plymouth Plantation*. In it, he said, "Out of small beginnings greater things have been produced by His hand that made all things of nothing . . . as one small candle may light a thousand, so the light here kindled hath shone unto many, yea in some sort to our whole nation."

Each life is like one small candle. When you capture transforming moments alone with God, you are refined into a person whose life counts now and into eternity. "Everything . . . finds its *purpose in him*" (Col. 1:15–18 MSG; emphasis added).

When we meet our heavenly Father at the end of life's earthly journey, we will want to say as Jesus did, "I have finished the work which You have given me to do" (John 17:4). Won't it be wonderful to hear Him say, "Well done," particularly when that "well done" has stemmed from being transformed during solitary refinement?

As we have seen, not only in my life, but in the lives of several others, marvelous, miraculous, and monumental things transpire when we enter God's holy presence—secret adventures, unusual direction, descriptive mandates, supernatural angels, unveiled mysteries, heavenly visions, and holy concepts that this world cannot even begin to comprehend.

—⚏—

In the tiny book of Jude, the brother of James, alone with God, penned shocking facts about fallen angels and Michael's contest with the devil; while the powerful book of Revelation, an astounding vision was received and written by John, the apostle, while captive and alone on the island of Patmos.

NOTES

CHAPTER 10: REVIVED RECEIVERS

1. Joyce Meyer, "Twelve Ways to Defeat the Devil" Radio Broadcast.

CHAPTER 11: DESTRUCTIVE DISTRACTIONS

1. Amy Grant and Chris Eaton, "Hats," *Hearts in Motion*, Sparrow, 1990.

2. John Lennon and Paul McCartney, "A Hard Day's Night," *A Hard Day's Night*, United Artists, 1964.

3. Susan Taylor, *Essence* (March 1994)

CHAPTER 14 NIPPING NEGATIVITY

1. Jack Canfield, quoted in Harvey Mackay, "Make 'Private Speech' Positive," *Tulsa World*, sec. E, January 21, 2007.

CHAPTER 17: LEADING THE LINE

1. Alanna Nash, "Lessons from Billy Graham," *Reader's Digest*, January 2007, 152–57.

2. A. W. Tozer, *The Pursuit of God* (Camp Hill, PA: Christian Publications, 1982), 76.

CHAPTER 19: GUARANTEED GREATNESS

1. Jim Croce, "Time in a Bottle," *You Don't Mess Around with Jim*, ABC, 1972.

ACKNOWLEDGMENTS

My adopted father, Peter Daniels, who inspires me to think bigger; Carol, my editor, who never fails to impress me; Justin, who pushed me to reach further by providing excellent research; John and Linda, who helped bring me to the dance; Victor, whose diligence caused things to happen; Thomas Nelson Inc., who made this book possible.

ABOUT THE AUTHOR

Dr. Robb Thompson has been a pastor for over twenty-five years. Though he earned his doctorate in theology at Life Christian University; and while he has authored over twenty books, has a television program, "Winning in Life," and has traveled the globe, speaking to audiences in over forty countries, what he most wants to be known for is his living witness to the goodness and love of God.

Dr. Thompson's path to God's best was not easy. He has weathered the storms of drugs, alcoholism, depression, and poverty. When he found God, he was in a mental institution, where he soon learned that the only way to fight the voices in his head was by speaking the Word of God. Today he is a living testament to how God's Word can renew a man's mind.

He is founder and pastor of Family Harvest Church, a growing congregation of over one thousand five hundred people in a suburb of Chicago. He founded International College of Excellence, a fully accredited school dedicated to helping people fulfill their call in ministry, and is the cofounder of Gabriel Call, an organization devoted to help build and develop Christian entrepreneurs.

His vision is simple: to influence people worldwide by equipping leaders in business, government, and ministry with practical-yet-life-changing principles for success. His mission is to inspire those he serves to pursue personal excellence and achievement because his life is evidence that with God, anything is possible.